Walking Together c
Anglican and Cathc
Official Commentaries on the
ARCIC Agreed Statement

The publication of this volume was made possible thanks to the generous support of the Malines Conversations Group

First published in Great Britain in 2018

Society for Promoting Christian Knowledge
36 Causton Street
London SW1P 4ST
www.spck.org.uk

The author and publisher have made every effort to ensure that the external website and email
addresses included in this book are correct and up to date at the time of going to press. The author
and publisher are not responsible for the content, quality or continuing accessibility of the sites.

British Library Cataloguing-in-Publication Data
A catalogue record for this book is available from the British Library

ISBN 978–0–281–07909–4
eBook ISBN 978–0–281–07895–0

Typeset by Fakenham Prepress Solutions, Fakenham, Norfolk NR21 8NL
First printed in Great Britain by Ashford Colour Press

eBook by Fakenham Prepress Solutions, Fakenham, Norfolk NR21 8NL

Produced on paper from sustainable forests

A Roman Catholic Commentary on *Walking Together on the Way: Learning to Be the Church—Local, Regional, Universal* of the Anglican–Roman Catholic International Commission

Ormond Rush
(Australian Catholic University)

Entitled *Walking Together on the Way: Learning to Be the Church—Local, Regional, Universal* (henceforth, *WTW*), this is the first Agreed Statement of the third phase of the Anglican–Roman Catholic International Commission (ARCIC III). The commentary that follows will situate *WTW* within the history of ARCIC, highlight its underlying ecclesiology and ecumenical methodology, summarize its salient points, and evaluate, from a Catholic perspective, its possible contribution to contemporary Roman Catholic self-understanding and practice. The commentary will refer to *WTW* as 'the document' or 'the Agreed Statement'. Its chapters will be referred to as 'sections', with their numbered elements as 'paragraphs' (§).

The Background

Since ARCIC was established in 1966 and began its work in 1970, there have been three major phases of dialogue. *WTW* is the result of the third major phase, which began in 2011. While the document builds upon the results of previous Agreed Statements from ARCIC I and ARCIC II, two Agreed Statements in particular have proved to be important, one from 1991 and the other from 1999. Firstly, the 1991 ARCIC II Agreed Statement *Church as Communion* provides the fundamental communion ecclesiology which *WTW* explicitly presupposes. In 1999, the third of ARCIC II's statements on authority, *The Gift of Authority*, brought further clarity to the issues around the notion of authority which emerge from a communion ecclesiology. This Agreed Statement ended with a list of questions that had been raised for Roman Catholics during the dialogue:

> [I]s there at all levels effective participation of clergy as well as lay people in emerging synodal bodies? Has the teaching of the Second Vatican Council regarding the collegiality of bishops been implemented sufficiently? Do the actions of bishops reflect sufficient awareness of the extent of the authority they receive through ordination for governing the local church? Has enough provision been made to ensure consultation between the Bishop of Rome and the local churches prior to the making of important decisions affecting either a local church or the whole Church? How is the variety of theological opinion taken into account when such decisions are made? In supporting the Bishop of Rome in his work of promoting communion among the churches, do the structures and procedures of the Roman Curia adequately respect the exercise of episcope at other levels? Above all, how will the Roman Catholic Church address the question of universal primacy as it emerges from 'the patient and fraternal dialogue' about the exercise of the office of the Bishop of Rome to which John Paul II has invited 'church leaders and their theologians'? (*The Gift of Authority*, §57)

These would turn out to be questions which ARCIC III set out to address, and the current document *WTW* is the result.

When ARCIC III was constituted in 2011, it was given the mandate to explore the double theme: 'The Church as Communion, local and universal, and how in communion the local and universal Church come to discern right ethical teaching.' When work began, the Commission deliberately chose to limit its focus initially to only the first of these, the Church as communion, local and universal, leaving the second matter of ethical teaching to a later document. However, as explained in paragraph 11, the Commission decided to broaden its focus beyond just the local and worldwide/universal levels of church life, and address the intermediate regional level.

The reason given by the Commission for this addition to its mandate is the simple *de facto* existence of regional structures in both communions. On the Catholic side, this is evident in the administrative organization of dioceses into regions, often national, with accompanying episcopal con-ferences; or at a smaller level, canon law's provision for metropolitans and provinces. Moreover, *WTW* recalls the regular practice of regional synods in the early Church and their 'utility' (§11); these regional bodies were found to be beneficial both at the local and at the universal levels, because of the opportunity they afforded for dialogue on common problems in church life, worship, and teaching. Citing the universal-level Council of Nicaea of 325 as a paradigmatic example of such benefits also on the regional level, the document asserts: 'At all times in the Church, from its earliest days to the present, controversy, debate, dialogue, and synodal processes have led—eventually and often not quickly—to clarification, and ultimately a more precise articulation of "the faith that was once for all entrusted to the saints" (Jude 1.3) … The development of doctrine shows that contested questions, often debated vigorously throughout the Church, locally, regionally, and globally, can lead eventually to a deeper common understanding and more precise articulation of the truth' (§12). These sentences could well summarize one major contribution that *WTW* might well make for the Catholic Church's renewed appreciation and promotion of regional levels of teaching and governance.

This present commentary is intended as a *Catholic* commentary on *WTW*, looking at only what the Roman Catholic Church has to learn; the Anglican Communion provides its own commentary, which considers the various suggested points of Anglican receptive learning from Catholics. How, then, can *WTW* be assessed from the point of view of the Roman Catholic Church? What criterion should be used? The fundamental criterion chosen here is the pre-eminent authority for Catholics in the recent magisterial teaching of the Roman Catholic Church, the Second Vatican Council (1962–65). This ecclesial event, along with its sixteen documents, has known over fifty years of reception into the fabric of the Church's life and self-understanding. Pope Francis is currently promoting an even deeper reception of the Council through his programme of renewal and reform. The question may well be raised: can *WTW* help Roman Catholics incorporate into their ecclesial life aspects of the Council's vision which have yet to be fully received?

The Ecclesiology

As ARCIC II's Agreed Statement *Church as Communion* shows, communion ecclesiology has been of great benefit in ecumenical dialogues, and ARCIC's own Agreed Statements in particular. *WTW* presupposes and builds on this ecclesiology. Paragraph 3 specifically names the document's ecclesiological emphasis: the interrelated notions of 'the Church as the pilgrim People of God' and 'the Church as communion (*koinonia*)'. These two ways of speaking of the Church fashion the document's vision. The biblical phrase 'People of God' appears seven times throughout. But it is the biblical and patristic notion of 'communion' that overwhelmingly predominates as *WTW*'s integrating principle. It is used 16 times in the introductory glossary for explaining other terms throughout the text; 18 times in the two-page preface; and 249 times in the main text (even apart from the 61 instances of the term 'Anglican Communion').

This ecclesiological framework certainly coheres with the self-understanding of the Roman Catholic Church as presented in the documents of the Second Vatican Council. More than any other characterization of the Church, the Second Vatican Council's documents most often refer to the Church as 'the People of God'. As used by the Council, the term refers to the whole body of the faithful: laity, religious, priests, bishops, Pope—together in relationship with the Triune God, who calls the whole Church on mission. The Council envisages the People of God bound together in unity by the Holy Spirit as a communion of all the faithful (*communio fidelium*), albeit living in local churches throughout the world, which together constitute a communion of churches (*communio ecclesiarum*); these churches are shepherded by bishops in communion with one another, with and under the Bishop of Rome (*communio hierarchica*). The 1985 Extraordinary Synod of Bishops, convened by Pope John Paul II twenty years after the Second Vatican Council, stated: 'The ecclesiology of communion is the central idea and the fundamental idea in the documents of the Council' (*Final Report*, II C).

In exploring the implications of communion ecclesiology, *WTW* uses some specific terminology. When speaking of the various dimensions of ecclesial communion (local, trans-local, regional, national, worldwide/universal), *WTW* uses the language of 'levels'. This usage, it states, is 'common ecumenical practice' (§10, note 4). The term 'trans-local' is used to refer to 'any expression of church life beyond the level of the diocese: that is to say, at the metropolitan, regional, national, and worldwide levels' (although there seems to be some inconsistency, with the terms 'trans-local' and 'regional' sometimes being used interchangeably). Because of the different nuances in Anglican and Catholic understanding, the descriptor 'worldwide' is used when referring to the former, and the descriptor 'universal' when referring to the latter.

Also, the document appropriates the Anglican term 'instruments of communion' to describe, for both traditions, 'structures, procedures, and ministries which serve to maintain the quality and reality of communion at the local, regional, and worldwide levels' (see the explanation of 'Instruments of communion' in 'Usage of Terms'). Importantly, *WTW* acknowledges that its deliberate focus on only 'structures and processes' (§14) is not intended to undervalue 'many other sources of influence on the shaping of church teaching, such as the tradition, the work of theologians, the lives and writings of the saints, and responses of Christians to societal evils' (§14). In other words, the ecclesiological vision of *WTW* is not intended to be simply juridical in its focus. Moreover, as the Co-Chairs of ARCIC III emphasize, *WTW*'s focus on 'instruments of communion' is intended to further the primary goal of 'visible unity and full ecclesial communion' sought in Anglican–Roman Catholic dialogue: 'The conviction is that by examining and reforming our respective instruments of communion alongside and in conversation with each other, we are also growing closer to each other and strengthening the imperfect communion that already exists between us' (Preface).

WTW's examination of the local, regional, and universal levels of communion in the Church draws upon two particular rubrics: (1) the four marks of the Church as one, holy, catholic, apostolic; and (2) the threefold office of Christ as prophet, priest, and king. These rubrics serve as investigative frameworks for examining points of commonality and difference and, together, provide coherence to the document's presentation.

Firstly, since both traditions profess the Nicene-Constantinopolitan Creed, each treasures the ecclesial attributes of unity, holiness, catholicity, and apostolicity. All four of these characteristics of the Church of Christ become in the document reference points for examining the need for conversion in one's own ecclesial life, and for possible receptive learning for both traditions. *WTW* shows how such possibilities for Catholic learning emerge in discussion of unity and catholicity, and apostolicity and holiness. For example, an emphasis on *unity* in the Church, so prized by Catholics, is balanced in Anglican practice with an appreciation of *diversity*. While diversity is also a quality officially affirmed by the Second Vatican Council in *Lumen Gentium* §13 as a dimension of *catholicity*, in Catholic practice a tendency to emphasize uniformity can at times prevail.

Secondly, the rubric of the threefold office of Christ as prophet, priest, and king is regularly referred to in the text. At the Second Vatican Council, this rubric provided the background for one of the Council's most significant shifts: its movement away from an exclusively hierarchical understanding of the Church to a primary understanding of the Church as the People of God, that is, the whole body of the faithful, including the ordained (bishops, priests, deacons). The first draft of the document on the Church presented to the bishops spoke of only the bishops as participating in the threefold office of Christ, as prophet, priest, king—referring to the teaching, sanctifying, and governing aspects of Christian life and mission. Chapter 2 of *Lumen Gentium* speaks of the whole body of the faithful participating in the three offices of Christ. *WTW* addresses mainly the teaching (prophetic) and governing (kingly) offices, at each of the three levels of communion.

These two rubrics serve as frameworks for examining points of commonality and difference on the issues of local, regional, and universal 'levels' of communion.

The Methodology

There are at least two ways in which *WTW* is different from previous ARCIC Agreed Statements: its employment of a 'receptive ecumenism' methodology; and the very typographical arrangement of the text.

For the first time, ARCIC adopts 'receptive ecumenism' as its explicit methodology for dialogue. As summarized by *WTW*, the process of receptive ecumenism 'involves being prepared both to discern what appears to be overlooked or underdeveloped in one's own tradition and to ask whether such things are better developed in the other tradition. It then requires the openness to ask how such perceived strengths in the other tradition might be able, through receptive learning, to help with the development and enrichment of this aspect of ecclesial life within one's own tradition' (§18). This spirit of openness captures what Cardinal Joseph Ratzinger has said of ecumenical dialogue: 'There is a duty to let oneself be purified and enriched by the other.'[1]

An important nuance that *WTW* brings to the application of receptive ecumenism is its emphasis on fraternal care (although it is not precisely named as such in the text): sharing a gift that the other may need is not a matter of proving who is right or better than the other, but rather, in Christian charity, of helping the other because they are in need and are experiencing 'tensions and difficulties' in their ecclesial life. This pervasive tone of care is captured in the very title of the document: *Walking Together on the Way*. Although this is not made explicit, there is a tone of mutual gratitude that characterizes the whole document. Also important in receptive ecumenism is the recognition that sometimes a different practice of the other tradition may not be judged to be of value, or to be of value in a different way.

Sections IV, V, and VI of the document in particular make explicit use of the method of receptive ecumenism. Each section follows the same pattern: (1) an exploration of the common heritage and shared understandings of both traditions; (2) an exploration of the tensions and difficulties that each is experiencing within its own life; and (3) an exploration of the possibilities which one tradition sees for itself if it were to appropriate what is a strength and grace in the life of the other. Here, differences can become graces, and sources of guidance from the Holy Spirit for addressing tensions and difficulties within one's own tradition. As paragraph 46 puts it: 'Anglicans and Catholics have some differing understandings, practices, and structures, as well as differences of vocabulary (see "Usage of Terms"). The aim here is not to eradicate these differences. *The point rather is to ask how each might be a resource for the other so that what is experienced as grace and benefit in one might help address what is less developed in the other*' (my italics).

The notion of 'receptive learning' illustrates the grace that the method of receptive ecumenism can be for the Roman Catholic Church. At the Second Vatican Council, triumphalism (along with clericalism and juridicism) was highlighted as a danger for the Catholic Church in a speech by Bishop Emile De Smedt at the end of the first session. The Council went on to offer a humbler Catholic ecclesial self-understanding. Its Decree

---

[1] 'Ecumenismo: crisi o svolta? Dialogo tra il Card. J. Ratzinger e il teologo protestante P. Ricca', *Nuova Umanità*, 15 (1993) 101–21, available at: www.cittanuova.it/cn-download/10730/10731.

on Ecumenism states as a general principle: 'It is hardly surprising if sometimes one tradition has come nearer than the other to an apt appreciation of certain aspects of the revealed mystery or has expressed them in a clearer manner. As a result, these various theological formulations are often to be considered as complementary rather than conflicting' (*Unitatis Redintegratio*, §17). Receptive ecumenism takes this general principle and proposes it as a method for ecumenical encounter. Receptive ecumenism invites each tradition in a dialogue to look humbly at the weaknesses and impasses in its own life, and to recognize perhaps that the other tradition lives out its life with different structures and processes that may well be gifts to be received.

All of this has resonances with particular emphases in the vision of Pope Francis. In speaking of the scandal of division among Christians and the call to Christian unity, he states: 'How many important things unite us! If we really believe in the abundantly free working of the Holy Spirit, we can learn so much from one another! It is not just about being better informed about others, but rather about reaping what the Spirit has sown in them, which is also meant to be a gift for us' (*Evangelii Gaudium*, §246). In their Common Declaration of 5 October 2016, Archbishop Justin Welby and Pope Francis implicitly allude to the methodology of receptive ecumenism when they state: 'We have become partners and companions on our pilgrim journey, facing the same difficulties, and strengthening each other by learning to value the gifts which God has given to the other, and to receive them as our own in humility and gratitude.' It was this image of 'partners and companions on our pilgrim journey' that gave rise to the title of the present Agreed Statement: *Walking Together on the Way*.

The Layout of the Document

The second way in which *WTW* is different from previous ARCIC Agreed Statements is in its physical (typographical) arrangement. This is not unimportant, and is related to the method of receptive ecumenism.

There are three kinds of page layout throughout the document. The first is where the paragraphs take up the whole width of page; such paragraphs generally examine a common heritage, something that both traditions continue to embody in their ecclesial life. The second is where there are *parallel* columns, side by side, with the left column treating Anglican belief or practice and the right column treating Catholic belief or practice; this arrangement provides a graphical way of presenting 'the similar but differentiated ways in which our respective structures seek to serve our communions' (Preface). The third arrangement is *sequential* paragraphs, but with those referring to Anglican belief or practice aligned to the left of the page and those referring to Catholic belief and practice on the right side of the page; this provides a graphical way of differentiating between what are 'quite different processes' (Preface) in the two traditions.

These three ways of presenting the text have the benefit of highlighting in a nuanced way the range of commonalities and differences, thus preparing the reader for the receptive learning from the other that might be possible between the two traditions.

The Content

After a glossary and then a Preface by the two Co-Chairs of ARCIC III, the main part of the document consists of six sections and a conclusion.

That the document begins with a glossary ('Usage of Terms') turns out to be useful. The reader is given prior information as to the special theological terms that will be used, as well as alerted to the differences and nuances in some of the language used by each tradition. The two Co-Chairs of the dialogue—one Anglican, one Roman Catholic—then provide a Preface. Importantly, they note the spirit of fraternal care that has pervaded the seven years of dialogue and has produced *WTW*. This spirit is captured in the document's title: 'The sense is of our two traditions each walking the pilgrim way in each other's company: "pilgrim companions", making their own journey of conversion into greater life but supported by the other as they do so.'

The first numbered section is an Introduction, which introduces the main theme of local, regional, and worldwide/universal levels of communion. After reminding the reader of the previous phases of ARCIC's work, this section situates *WTW* along the trajectory of previous Agreed Statements. A brief survey of the distinctive histories of the two traditions highlights the way in which regional levels of teaching and governance became important in the Anglican tradition, while a universalist approach came to dominate in the Roman Catholic tradition. Importantly too, the Introduction discusses positive and negative 'signs of the times' (although the actual phrase is not used) which challenge both traditions in their mission in a contemporary globalized and secular world. The hope is expressed that facing these common challenges together, and recognizing the different gifts that each tradition brings to that task, may provide opportunities for learning for both sides. The ultimate goal is a more effective proclamation of the Gospel of salvation, through a more effective realization of local, regional, and universal levels of ecclesial life.

Section II focuses on 'The Church Local and Universal in the Apostolic and Post-Apostolic Periods'. This is a critical section, given the authoritative role that Scripture and the writings of the Patristic period have for both traditions. Some accents can be selected. The section shows how the New Testament witnesses to the felt need of local churches to refer to and draw upon the resources of other local churches. The Holy Spirit is mentioned twenty-one times throughout the section, especially in discussion of the Lucan writings. Significantly, the document notes in paragraph 34 how the letters of the New Testament speak of 'apostolicity' in pragmatic terms: 'In these epistles the apostles are often seen delegating their authority to local leaders (Acts 11.30; 14.23; 15.2, 4, 6, 22, 23; 16.4; 20.17; 21.18; 1 Tim 5.17, 19; Tit 1.5; Jas 5.14; 1 Pet 5.1).' Examination of the book of Revelation brings to the fore an important point on the matter of diversity: each of the seven churches of Asia Minor is presented as a particular means through which the one Christ is revealed in the Spirit: 'To each is shown a distinctive facet of Christ's glory (2.1; 2.8; 2.12; 2.18; 3.1; 3.7; 3.14). To each is given a distinctive message as to how better to reflect the light of that glory. Moreover, the need for repentance in these distinctive local churches is frequently repeated (2.5; 2.16; 2.22; 3.3; 3.19). In each case, they are encouraged to "listen to what the Spirit is saying to the churches" (3.22)' (§37). The section goes on to note important historical developments in the teaching and governance of the early Church as it expanded and responded to new exigencies: the emergence of a 'rule of faith'; of creeds; of bishops, presbyters, and deacons; of the primacy of the Bishop of Rome; of regional and ecumenical councils.

Section III moves from the previous section's examination of the foundational Christian tradition to presenting elements of a systematic overview of the theme under review. Titled 'Ecclesial Communion in Christ: The Need for Effective Instruments of Communion', it sets out to outline the 'shared ecclesiology' (§62) of both traditions by presenting 'the fundamentals of a theology of ecclesial communion' (§20). This rich summary of key points draws upon not only previous Agreed Statements, especially *Church as Communion* and *The Gift of Authority*, but also wider ecumenical dialogue statements, such as the World Council of Churches' Faith and Order paper *The Church: Towards a Common Vision*.

From the outset, the very notion of communion is shown to exclude any unbalanced view that would promote the isolated importance of one of the 'two poles, local and trans-local' (§48). Both excessive demands for autonomy by the local and excessive demands for centralization by the trans-local endanger genuine communion.

Appropriately, the section presents the shared Anglican and Roman Catholic belief that baptism and eucharist are the sacramental means of initiation into ecclesial communion in Christ through the Spirit. In other words, ecclesial communion is founded on baptismal and eucharistic communion. Baptism, as incorporation into Christ, enables all the baptized to participate in the three offices of Christ as prophet, priest, and king. This participation by all the faithful means there must be interrelationship between all levels of the Church, local, and trans-local. Furthermore, through baptism the Holy Spirit bestows on all the baptized and on the Church as a whole 'an instinct for the faith' (*sensus fidei fidelium*), which guarantees that the Church will never fail in its believing. Just like the participation by all in the threefold office, this participation by all in the *sensus fidelium* through the Holy Spirit means there must be interrelationship between all levels of the Church, local and trans-local. Just as *Lumen Gentium* (§13) emphasized the catholicity of the Church as a unity-in-diversity, so too *WTW* sees 'instruments of communion' at all levels of the Church as vital for maintaining both legitimate unity and legitimate diversity throughout the worldwide Church, by promoting local and regional inculturation of the faith. 'The task of instruments of communion is to serve the unity and the diversity—the catholicity—of the Church' (§57).

From baptism, the section moves to explore the eucharistic dimension of ecclesial communion: 'Anglicans and Catholics hold that the communion entered into in baptism reaches its sacramental fullness in the celebration of the eucharist' (§58). The eucharist makes Christ sacramentally present throughout the world, at all levels. By its very nature, eucharistic participation is 'necessarily collective and ecclesial' (§59). For both Anglicans and Roman Catholics this ecclesial communion is symbolized most clearly when a local community gathers in eucharist around its bishop.

The section concludes by noting certain differences between the two traditions which will feature in the later discussion: the distinctive understandings of the roles played by the Archbishop of Canterbury and the Bishop of Rome; the levels at which ecumenical agreements are approved or binding decisions can be made; the very question of 'priority' of local over trans-local levels, and vice versa.

Sections IV, V, and VI then treat the three levels separately: the local, the regional, and the worldwide/universal. Here we come to the core of *WTW*'s contribution: on each of these levels, there are common understandings that should augur well for sensitivity in appreciating any difference; there is by each of the two traditions an honest and humble acknowledgement of tensions and difficulties that it is currently experiencing in its own life; and, most importantly, there is a recognition that the Holy Spirit may have developed in the other tradition (before or since the English Reformation) 'instruments of communion' that the other might well learn from when addressing their own tensions and difficulties.

Importantly, Section IV begins with the 'local': 'Instruments of Communion at the Local Levels of Anglican and Catholic Life'. These various local levels, from the parish to the diocese, constitute 'the reality of the Church as it is most widely experienced' (§80). Here both traditions make use of the ancient rubric of the *tria munera* of Christ for understanding life and ministry at these various local levels, as well as making use of similar local structures and ministries, such as parish, diocese, bishop, presbyter, and deacon. The bishop here is especially valued by both as an important authoritative instrument of communion.

However, despite these commonalities, each tradition experiences in its own way certain tensions and difficulties. Common to both at the local level is the danger of 'parochialism', a myopic view that isolates the local in importance to the detriment of any wider connection with other ecclesial communities. The Agreed Statement brings to the fore a significant lack in the Roman Catholic vision and practice: 'The canon law of the Latin Church currently describes the universal Church and the local churches and the relevant structures and procedures pertaining at these levels but gives relatively little attention to the regional level' (§108). Another of the tensions and difficulties Roman Catholics acknowledge is that, despite the Second Vatican Council's affirmation that the laity participate in the three offices of Christ, in reality, at the local levels, such participation has yet to reach full potential. While there has been, since the Council, 'a burgeoning of lay participation' (§83), lay people at best are allowed a merely *consultative* role in decision-making, with canon law not even requiring such consultation as mandatory. Anglican structures, on the other hand, provide for a *deliberative* role for lay people (they participate in decision-making). Even the selection of bishops involves lay participation. Anglicans too demand of the local bishop a dialogic approach to oversight; they speak of 'the "bishop-in-synod"' (§90). Within this pervasive dialogic ethos, a particular Anglican value highlighted by *WTW* is the welcome given to open debate, which the document acknowledges is something that a Roman Catholic emphasis on unity and universal oversight can downplay, resulting in 'the suppression of difference, the inhibiting of candid conversation, and the avoidance of contentious issues in open fora' (§96). In all these areas, possibilities for receptive learning present themselves to the Roman Catholic Church.

Section V moves to intermediate levels of communion: 'Instruments of Communion at the Regional Levels of Anglican and Roman Catholic Life'. Instances of Roman Catholic regional bodies and offices are: provinces, metropolitan archbishops, episcopal conferences, wider geographical federations of episcopal conferences, regional synods of bishops, and particular councils (provincial and plenary councils). The document notes the ancient precedent of instruments of communion at the regional level, involving participation at times beyond just clerics. Local churches in the early Church did not pretend to be self-sufficient; on various issues, they depended on the wisdom and support of surrounding churches. A central insight, therefore, of this section of *WTW* is that concerted effort at the regional levels is necessary and beneficial for local churches, and yet with implications for universal communion. Thus *WTW* rightly highlights the ecclesial value of distinctively regional issues: 'Not every issue touches everyone in the world, and thus not every issue that affects more than one local church requires deliberation at the worldwide/universal level, which exists to treat issues that affect all' (§107). However, regional decisions do have an impact on the bonds of communion beyond the region.

More than for the local or worldwide levels, *WTW* at this point notes an 'asymmetry' (§108) between the two traditions when comparing and contrasting them: 'On account of the history and development of provincial churches, Anglicans invest greater ecclesiological significance in the regional level than the Roman Catholic Church currently does. The canon law of the Latin Church currently describes the universal Church and the local churches and the relevant structures and procedures pertaining at these levels but gives relatively little attention to the regional level' (§108). Anglican worldwide expansion through the agency of British colonialism means that in a post-colonial world Anglicans are sensitive to the independence of new provinces, each with its own regional structure of doctrinal oversight and governance. For Roman Catholics, partly because of their suspicion of national churches in the early modern and modern periods, little authority has been afforded to regional structures, and the centralized authority of the Pope (and Roman Curia) predominated in the Catholic imagination until the Second Vatican Council. Exploration of this asymmetry leads ARCIC III to present in *WTW* some of its most helpful possibilities for Roman Catholic receptive learning. For example, affording greater authority to episcopal conferences as regional instruments of communion within the centralized ethos of the Roman Catholic Church is highlighted as a particular instance where Catholic receptive learning can take place, as is the lack of opportunities for open dialogue that involves priests, deacons, and lay people in any deliberative way.

Section VI discusses 'Instruments of Communion at the Worldwide/ Universal Level of Anglican and Roman Catholic Life'. Despite the conviction concerning the need for unity in the faith throughout the world, the difference in terminology regarding instruments of communion at this level reflects nuances in the approaches of the two traditions, each with strengths and weaknesses. For Anglicans, the word 'worldwide' refers to four instruments of communion: the Lambeth Conference, the Archbishop of Canterbury, the Anglican Consultative Council, and the Primates' Meeting. For Roman Catholics, the word 'universal', when referring to instruments of communion, generally applies to the four major instruments: an ecumenical council of all bishops, the Bishop of Rome, the Roman Curia, and the international synods of bishops. In reality, however, each of these instruments operates with certain tensions and difficulties, with demands for greater autonomy on matters directly related to local and regional issues.

The Conclusion, 'Growing Together into the Fullness of Christ', emphasizes that a common sense of urgency has driven the dialogue: since 'church structures support the mission of the Church' (§151), any opportunity to make those structures more effective should be welcomed. The humility to do so has characterized the receptive ecumenism which has guided the work of ARCIC III. Since the Holy Spirit has been at work in both traditions since their separation, for each tradition the instruments of communion developed by the other in its subsequent history may well be 'tokens of divine providence' (§152), which the Spirit is inviting it to embrace.

Across all three levels of communion—local, regional, and universal—*WTW* raises possibilities for Roman Catholic receptive learning from the Anglican tradition. Since some of these touch on more than one level, these learnings will now be evaluated together.

The Resonances

WTW can be best evaluated by reading its 'proposals for mutual receptive learning' (§155) alongside the renewal and reform vision of the Second Vatican Council, and Pope Francis's current attempts to inculcate that vision more deeply into Catholic life. As noted earlier, the Second Vatican Council is the pre-eminent authority for Catholics in the recent magisterial teaching of the Roman Catholic Church. Of it, Pope Francis has written: 'The Church feels a great need to keep this event alive. With the Council, the Church entered a new phase of her history' (*Misericordiae Vultus*, §4). Pope John Paul II had called the Council 'a sure compass by which to take our bearings in the century now beginning' (*Novo Millennio Ineunte*, §57). Accordingly, this commentary now assesses the major proposals of *WTW*, employing the 'compass' of the Second Vatican Council.

However, a nuanced understanding of the vision of Vatican II is required. Pope Paul VI noted in his address to the bishops on the last working day of the Council: 'quite a few questions raised during the course of the council itself still await appropriate answer'.[2] The Council did not attempt to provide systematic treatises on every issue it treated. As Walter Kasper has pointed out: 'The synthesis brought about by the last council was highly superficial, and in no way satisfactory. But then it is not the function of councils to draw up theological syntheses. A council presents the indispensable "frame of reference". The synthesis is then a matter for the theology that comes afterwards.'[3]

This is directly pertinent to the themes that *WTW* addresses: the local, regional, and universal levels of ecclesial communion. The Second Vatican Council does not present a comprehensive synthesis of all aspects of those issues, nor did it attempt to do so. Its communion ecclesiology was only inchoate. The Council certainly presents a fresh, new theology of the local church; it addresses previous imbalances regarding papal and episcopal roles across the universal Church; it (albeit briefly) addresses the importance of regional structures such as synods and episcopal conferences; above all, through a developing communion ecclesiology, it presents the Church as the People of God, the *universitas fidelium* (as a *communio fidelium*), dispersed in local churches throughout the world (as a *communio ecclesiarum*), to whom the hierarchy, with and under the Bishop of Rome, is called to serve (as a *communio hierarchica*).

---

2   Pope Paul VI, 'Closing Address: Fourth Session', in *Council Daybook: Vatican II, Session 4*, ed. Floyd Anderson (Washington, DC: National Catholic Welfare Conference, 1966), pp. 359–62, at p. 359.

3   Walter Kasper, 'The Church as Communion: Reflections on the Guiding Ecclesiological Idea of the Second Vatican Council', in *Theology and Church* (New York: Crossroad, 1989), pp. 148–65, at p. 158. A synthesis of the vision of the Second Vatican Council is to be found by attending to the complex debates throughout the Council regarding the drafting of its documents, as well as reading together, as a whole, the sixteen documents which it promulgated.

Some issues remain in tension in the conciliar documents. For example, affirmation of the participation of all the faithful in the three offices of Christ is not given effective structural support. Regarding the prophetic office in particular, the whole People of God's *infallibility in believing* (because of the Holy Spirit's gift to all of a *sensus fidei*) and the bishops' and Pope's *infallibility in teaching* (because of their possession of a 'sure charism of truth', *Dei Verbum*, §8) are teachings left in tension by the Council, without the provision of any institutional structures throughout the world Church which could facilitate two-way dialogue between *the whole People* and the Pope and bishops. Certainly, while they provide many of the elements, the conciliar documents do not provide any systematic presentation of communion ecclesiology at the local, regional, and universal levels. The Council, for example, does not give much attention to the regional level in the teaching and governing aspects of church life. Rather, the two poles of local and universal can tend to dominate, depending on the topic at hand, with only suggestive openings indicated for a more comprehensive ecclesiology. Here, as on other topics, the Council provided only trajectories pointing towards a synthesis. Nevertheless, while there are these lacunae in the documents of the Second Vatican Council, they can be illuminated and a synthesis unveiled—when the Council's comprehensive vision is taken into account. And this is true with regard to an integrated theology of the Council's vision concerning ecclesial communion at the local, regional, and universal levels. Here Pope Francis is playing a direct role.

The Second Vatican Council clearly, for Pope Francis, is his 'compass'. In drawing the elements of its vision into a comprehensive synthesis for the twenty-first century, he wants to highlight in that vision the importance of the local and the regional, without downplaying the default emphasis on the universal in the Roman Catholic imagination. The Council divided its attention between renewing and reforming the inner life of the Church (*ad intra*) and re-invigorating the outward thrust of the Church (*ad extra*). There are several emphases in Pope Francis's synthesis of both those thrusts: a missionary Church; a poor Church for the poor; a Church without clericalism; an ecologically converted Church; and so on. Following the Second Vatican Council, the Pope wants to balance the *ad intra* and *ad extra* energies of the Church, seeing the latter however as the main game.

Certain highlights of the Pope Francis's integration of the Second Vatican Council's vision of the Church *ad intra* have remarkable parallels with the accents of *WTW*. The Co-Chairs' Preface for *WTW* already refers to 'Pope Francis's call for a fully synodal Church in accord with the vision of the Second Vatican Council', as laid out in the Pope's programmatic 'Address Commemorating the 50th Anniversary of the Institution of the Synod of Bishops' (17 October 2015).[4] Here the Pope refers to a synodality that reaches to the very basic levels of church life, in order to 'listen to what the Spirit is saying to the churches' (Rev 2.7). He is using the term 'synodality' to bring to synthesis the Second Vatican Council's vision of the Church *ad intra*. We could call it his 'synodal communion ecclesiology' (although he does not use that exact term).

The Second Vatican Council does not once use the Latin equivalent of 'synodality', nor that of 'synodal'. But, as Pope Francis sees it, these terms capture precisely the comprehensive conciliar vision of the Church *ad intra*—from the Pope 'to the last of the lay faithful' (*Lumen Gentium*, §12, quoting St Augustine). 'Synodality' is his catch-all phrase for how he believes the Second Vatican Council is envisioning the Church *ad intra*— in its inner workings—without wanting to separate the Church's inner life from the effectiveness of its outward (*ad extra*) mission in the world. For Pope Francis, 'synodality' is more than just an element of a papal primacy and an episcopal collegiality exercised more collaboratively; he speaks of '*episcopal collegiality* within an entirely synodal Church'. And to emphasize the difference, he immediately repeats his distinction between the 'two different phrases: "episcopal collegiality" and an "entirely synodal Church"'.[5]

WTW's three levels of communion—local, regional, universal—are explicit elements in the Pope's vision. 'Synodality is a constitutive element of the Church. In this Church, as in an inverted pyramid, the top is located beneath the base.' 'A synodal Church', he says, 'is a Church which listens, which realizes that listening "is more than simply hearing". It is a mutual listening in which everyone has something to learn. The faithful people, the college of bishops, the Bishop of Rome: all listening to each other, and all listening to the Holy Spirit, the "Spirit of truth" (*Jn* 14:17), in order to know what [the Spirit] "says to the Churches" (*Rev* 2:7).'[6] He then talks of how this listening to the Spirit is a process that necessarily

---

[4] Pope Francis, Address Commemorating the 50th Anniversary of the Institution of the Synod of Bishops, 17 October 2015 (hereafter cited in footnotes as 'Address, 17 October 2015'), available at: http://w2.vatican.va/content/francesco/en/speeches/2015/october/documents/papa-francesco_20151017_50-anniversario-sinodo.html.

[5] Address, 17 October 2015.

[6] *Ibid.* The Pope is quoting here his own document *Evangelii Gaudium*, §171, along with Jn 14.17; Rev 2.7.

begins at the *local* level, and finds further ratification and synthesis at the *regional* level, and then reception by the whole Church (all the churches in communion) at the universal level, specifically through the instrument of the Synod of Bishops. Such a synodal Church, he says, requires effective institutional structures for listening to and determining the *sensus fidelium*. As the Pope notes, synodal structures already exist in canon law for listening to the faithful, from the parish, diocesan, national, regional, and international levels.[7] But these structures need to be further realized, not so much simply as papal and episcopal structures for governing and teaching the peripheries, but also as structures for enabling genuine participation by the peripheries in the governing and teaching of the whole Church.

'The Synod process *begins by listening to the people of God*, which "shares also in Christ's prophetic office", according to a principle dear to the Church of the first millennium: "*Quod omnes tangit ab omnibus tractari debet* [what affects everyone must be deliberated by everyone]".[8] Like *WTW*, Pope Francis speaks of different 'levels' in this ecclesial listening. 'The first level of the exercise of *synodality*' is the listening that happens within *local* churches in 'organs of communion', such as the presbyteral council, the college of consultors, chapters of canons, the pastoral council, and the diocesan synod. That these 'organs of communion' are listening to the whole People of God at the local level, especially the laity, is implied. 'The second level' of listening happens at the level of ecclesiastical provinces and regions, particular councils, and conferences of bishops. Renewal of these 'intermediary instances of *collegiality*' is needed if they are to be genuine antennae of synodal listening. And 'the last level' is the level of the universal Church, where the Synod of Bishops is 'the point of convergence of this listening process conducted at every level of the Church's life'. It is 'an expression of *episcopal collegiality* within an entirely synodal Church'. Importantly, this centripetal movement from local to international structures is not an attempt at greater centralization. 'The papacy and the central structures of the universal Church also need to hear the call to pastoral conversion ... Excessive centralization, rather than proving helpful, complicates the Church's life and her missionary outreach' (*Evangelii Gaudium*, §32).

---

7 Address, 17 October 2015. On these canonical structures specifically as instruments for listening to and discerning the *sensus fidelium*, see Anthony Ekpo, *The Breath of the Spirit in the Church: Sensus Fidelium and Canon Law* (Strathfield: St Pauls Publications, 2014).

8 Address, 17 October 2015. The Pope is quoting *Lumen Gentium*, §12.

The Challenges

The reception of the Second Vatican Council is far from complete. Many of its principles have yet to be incorporated fully into church life *ad intra* and *ad extra*. Several of the problematic areas in that reception process over the last fifty years have in fact been raised by *WTW*. Its proposals for a Catholic receptive learning from Anglicans may well provide help. Several of these proposals can be selected as particularly urgent and challenging. The challenges selected here are: (1) a greater recognition of the Holy Spirit working at all levels of the Church; (2) a greater recognition of diversity within a genuine catholicity; (3) a move towards less centralized structures of teaching and governance; (4) a greater deliberative authority afforded to regional structures such as episcopal conferences; (5) a greater participation of lay people; (6) the active promotion of genuine dialogue in the Church; (7) a greater appreciation of 'provisionality' and the continuing guidance of the Holy Spirit.

1. Greater Recognition of the Holy Spirit Working at All Levels of the Church

Appropriating *WTW*'s proposals, firstly, may help the Roman Catholic Church to better appreciate that the need to find better structural instruments of communion at all levels is, above all, for the sake of a better listening to the guidance of the Holy Spirit in its life. Throughout the four years of its meeting, the Second Vatican Council itself had an experience of receptive learning from the Catholic and Orthodox Eastern bishops and observers, who reminded the bishops that their evolving documents often were lacking appropriate emphasis on the Third Person of the Trinity in the life of the Church. The Council moved towards a greater appreciation of the role of the Holy Spirit. In the fifty years of the Council's reception, it is a sensibility that has yet to touch all aspects of Catholic life.

As an aside, while *WTW* presents a balanced Christology and pneumatology in its formulation of ecclesial communion, it too fails to give a consistent pneumatological emphasis. In its *ressourcement* of the tradition (see §§3 and 19), and in its systematic proposal of a communion ecclesiology, the document foregrounds the indispensable activity of the Holy Spirit in the life of the Church. In Section II's examination of the biblical and Patristic tradition, there are eighteen mentions of the presence, guidance, and power of the Holy Spirit in the early Christian communities (strangely, only one reference is made to the antiphonal evocation in the book of Revelation, 'Listen to what the Spirit is saying to the churches', which occurs seven times in the book). Then Section III, on communion ecclesiology, brings to the fore the origins of the Church in the Triune God, and the missions of the Word and the Spirit in the economy of salvation. The Spirit is here mentioned fourteen times. However, surprisingly, this pneumatological emphasis is diminished in the next three (central) sections, on the local, regional, and universal levels, where there is hardly any mention of the Spirit. Section IV, on the local level, certainly has three instances. But in Section V, concerning the regional level, there is no mention at all of the Holy Spirit. And in Section VI on the universal level, there is only one mention of the Holy Spirit, and that relates to 'recognizing the presence of the Spirit in other Christians, their churches, and their communities' (§149). Thus, there is nothing on the Holy Spirit working through diverse cultural expressions of the faith throughout the worldwide communion of churches (something that the documents of the Second Vatican Council does in several ways). *WTW*'s Conclusion does go on to mention the Holy Spirit three times. Admittedly, these central sections concern institutional instruments of communion at these three levels, and the pneumatological presuppositions had already been laid out in Sections II and III. In particular, the ecclesial task of 'listening to what the Spirit is saying to the churches' had been emphasized in the previous section, and it may not have seemed necessary to keep repeating that this is one important aspect of what is going on at these three levels of communion. However, the diminished focus on the Holy Spirit working through regional and universal levels of communion seems to be a missed opportunity.

In the formal documents and daily homilies of Pope Francis, there is regular mention of the indispensable role the Holy Spirit plays in bringing to realization the power and presence of Christ. When giving prominence in Sections II and III to a pneumatological ecclesiology, *WTW* emphasizes the importance for both traditions of *sensus fidei* in the Spirit's guidance of the Church in its ongoing reception of revelation. This too is a regular theme in Pope Francis's vision; in particular, he has often cited the reference in *Lumen Gentium* (§12) to the *sensus fidei* of the whole Church (see *Evangelii Gaudium*, §119, and his 17 October 2015 address on synodality). Strangely, *WTW* does not explicitly emphasize that the gift of *sensus fidei* is *a gift of the Holy Spirit* to all the baptized and to the whole Church of Christ, although it is alluded to in reference to the Church's indefectibility (§53). This is another missed opportunity for explicitly linking the means by which the Holy Spirit is at work at all levels of communion.

Notwithstanding these missed opportunities in *WTW*, the document importantly presents a challenge to the Roman Catholic Church to promote its instruments of communion as vehicles of the Holy Spirit speaking through all the faithful.

2. Greater Recognition of Diversity within a Genuine Catholicity

Just as the Roman Catholic Church can learn ways of being more attentive to the Holy Spirit, so too can it learn from the Anglican tradition a richer realization of catholicity as a unity in diversity. Certainly, while *Lumen Gentium* (§13) presented an ideal picture of a Catholicism which appreciates the diversity between churches (e.g. between the Latin churches and the Eastern churches), the Latin Church itself can fail to permit such diversity within its own local churches. *WTW* gives multiple examples of how the Anglican tradition permits and celebrates such diversity.

3. A Move towards Less Centralized Structures of Teaching and Governance

Similarly, and related to the issue of diversity, is the danger of over-centralization in the Roman Catholic Church. *WTW* notes that this can be related to a universalist ecclesiology which undervalues the local and the regional. As noted above, this is something that Pope Francis too has noted: 'I am conscious of the need to promote a sound "decentralization"' (*Evangelii Gaudium*, §16). While *WTW* speaks of the opposite danger of 'parochialism' (§93), such parochialism has had little opportunity to assert itself in recent Roman Catholic history. As Pope Francis attempts to address over-centralization, the more devolved models of teaching and governance in the Anglican Communion can only but provide practical examples to test out. As *WTW* states it: there is a difference between 'centralization' and 'being genuinely universal' (§143).

4. Greater Deliberative Authority Afforded to Regional Structures such as Episcopal Conferences

A matter related to the issue of over-centralization, also highlighted by *WTW*, is the lack of appropriate instruments of communion at the regional level in the Roman Catholic Church. That this is an area where learning from Anglicans can especially take place shows the need for a renewed Catholic theology and practice regarding the teaching and governance authority of episcopal conferences for limited matters of faith and discipline, albeit in communion with other churches, with the oversight of the Bishop of Rome. As *WTW* puts it: 'the Roman Catholic Church might fruitfully learn from the Anglican practice of provincial diversity and the associated recognition that on some matters different parts of the Communion can appropriately make different discernments influenced by cultural and contextual appropriateness' (§148).

This is something too that Pope Francis is urging. In his apostolic exhortation *Evangelii Gaudium* (§32), he refers to Pope John Paul II's encyclical *Ut Unum Sint*, where the previous Pope expressed an ecumenical openness to finding a way of exercising papal primacy 'in a new situation'. Pope Francis observes that further work needs to be done in this area, mentioning in particular episcopal conferences:

> *We have made little progress in this regard. The papacy and the central structures of the universal Church also need to hear the call to pastoral conversion. The Second Vatican Council stated that, like the ancient patriarchal Churches, episcopal conferences are in a position 'to contribute in many and fruitful ways to the concrete realization of the collegial spirit' [Lumen Gentium, §23]. Yet this desire has not been fully realized, since a juridical status of episcopal conferences which would see them as subjects of specific attributions, including genuine doctrinal authority, has not yet been sufficiently elaborated [Apostolos Suos]. Excessive centralization, rather than proving helpful, complicates the Church's life and her missionary outreach.*

The Pope refers in the above passage to the *motu proprio* of Pope John Paul II, *Apostolos Suos* ('On the Theological and Juridical Nature of Episcopal Conferences'), implying that the perspectives presented in this *motu proprio* needed further reflection. *Apostolos Suos* had given episcopal conferences limited authority, with conditions such as unanimous approval and a *recognitio* by the Apostolic See. Since *Apostolos Suos*, there has been much theological and canonical debate on whether this *motu proprio* has been too restrictive in interpreting the intention of the Second Vatican Council on the matter. *WTW* rightly observes, therefore, in its treatment of Catholic experience at the regional level of 'tensions and difficulties' (the title of sub-section V.B): 'The Roman Catholic Church struggles to articulate a formal theological basis for the nature and extent of the teaching authority of episcopal conferences in relation to the ordinary (non–defining) teaching magisterium of the Church' (§116).

Many of these sensibilities of *WTW* parallel those of Pope Francis. In taking the whole of the Council's vision of the Church *ad intra*, particularly with his notion of 'synodality', the Pope clearly wishes to strengthen particularly the regional level of episcopal conferences in terms of governance and teaching. As noted in *WTW*, the Pope's habit of citing texts promulgated by regional conferences of bishops (e.g. in *Laudato Si'* and *Amoris Laetitia*) is an implicit acknowledgement of their *de facto* authority (§111). For Pope Francis: 'It is not advisable for the Pope to take the place of local Bishops in the discernment of every issue which arises in their territory. In this sense, I am conscious of the need to promote a sound "decentralization"' (*Evangelii Gaudium*, §16).

With his comprehensive notion of synodality, Pope Francis is re-imagining regional structures such as episcopal conferences in terms of an ecclesial 'listening' that begins at the local level, is discerned at the regional level, and is discerned and acted upon at the universal level. An example of his firm intent in this matter is his recent *motu proprio* called *Magnum Principium*, which returns oversight of liturgical translations to episcopal conferences, as envisaged by the Second Vatican Council's constitution *Sacrosanctum Concilium*. Such regional decisions by an episcopal conference will now require only a simple *confirmatio* by the appropriate authority in the Roman Curia, and not the more controlling *recognitio*, which would allow that authority to change the local translation. This is a significant step towards giving episcopal conferences more deliberative decision-making authority in matters relevant to specific regions.

5. Greater Participation of Lay People

WTW notes the lack of Catholic structures for involving lay people, religious, and clergy in deliberative decision-making. The Second Vatican Council had affirmed the necessary participation of all the faithful (bishops, priests, deacons, religious, lay) in the mission of the Church. A corollary of that affirmation is the participation of all the faithful in the three offices of Christ (i.e. in the teaching, sanctifying, and governing areas of church life). However, the full implications of such teaching have yet to find structural support in the Roman Catholic Church, as *WTW* points out. Roman Catholic canon law currently provides no place for the mandatory participation of lay people in 'deliberative' decision-making at any of the three levels of communion. The Anglican tradition, on the other hand, gives more than lip-service to the role of laity in the areas of teaching and governance, providing for the mandatory involvement of the laity in deliberative decision-making at all levels of ecclesial life. Therefore, the proposals for Catholic receptive learning from Anglicans which *WTW* presents for the Church's consideration are yet one more opportunity for a more faithful reception of the vision of the Second Vatican Council regarding lay participation in all levels of church life, *ad intra* and *ad extra*.

6. Active Promotion of Genuine Dialogue in the Church

Related to the matter of lay participation, *WTW* foregrounds the importance of dialogue in the Church. Deep theological value is afforded by the Second Vatican Council to the *sensus fidei* of all the baptized (*Lumen Gentium*, §12); through this sense of the faithful, the Spirit speaks. It is therefore a source to be listened to: 'Listen to what the Spirit is saying to the churches' (Rev 2.7, etc.) The word 'dialogue' was a leitmotif used during the Council debates and throughout the documents it promulgated. During the Council, Pope Paul VI's encyclical *Ecclesiam Suam* had promoted the Church as a community of dialogue. *Gaudium et Spes* (§92) went on to speak of four concentric circles of dialogue the Church should promote: within the Church, with other Christians, with other believers, and with non-believers and the world at large. Regarding dialogue within the Church, it states:

> *[The mission of the Church] requires in the first place that we foster within the Church herself mutual esteem, reverence and harmony, through the full recognition of lawful diversity. Thus all those who compose the one People of God, both pastors and the general faithful, can engage in dialogue with ever abounding fruitfulness. For the bonds which unite the faithful are mightier than anything dividing them. Hence, let there be unity in what is necessary; freedom in what is unsettled, and charity in any case.*

While much progress has been made in the other three areas of dialogue, the matter of dialogue within the Church, in the way the Council is here envisioning, is far from being realized. Since the Council, the default position has prevailed, despite the Council's urgings; as *WTW* observes: '[The Catholic] instinct for unity can, however, result in the suppression of difference, the inhibiting of candid conversation, and the avoidance of contentious issues in open fora' (§96).

What has been generally looked upon with suspicion in the current ethos of the Roman Catholic Church is a major strength in the Anglican ethos: its genuine appreciation of 'open and sometimes painful debate' (§101) at all levels: local, regional, worldwide. As *WTW* points out, such open debate has nevertheless been promoted by Pope Francis himself, which augurs well for the official reception of *WTW*'s proposals by the Roman Catholic Church. In his greeting to the bishops at the start of the 2014 synod, Pope Francis spoke of a 'general and basic condition' for genuine synodality: the freedom to speak honestly. 'It is necessary to say with *parrhesia* [boldness] all that one feels.'[9] However, this must be

---

[9] Greeting of Pope Francis to the Synod Fathers during the First General Congregation of the

accompanied, he said, by another condition: listening with humility and with an open heart to what others say with honesty, what he calls 'the gift of listening'.[10] '*Synodality* is exercised with these two approaches.'

The creation of opportunities for open debate and the promotion of a willingness to listen to viewpoints contrary to one's own are therefore vital. In one of the more striking passages in *Evangelii Gaudium*, Francis appeals to the image of a polyhedron.[11] It appears in his discussion of one of his favourite axioms: 'the whole is greater than the part, but it is also greater than the sum of its parts' (*Evangelii Gaudium*, §235). He makes a distinction between two possible models for understanding this relationship. The first is a *sphere*, 'which is no greater than its parts, where every point is equidistant from the centre, and there are no differences between them' (*Evangelii Gaudium*, §236). He rejects this model. His preferred model is the *polyhedron*, 'which reflects the convergence of all its parts, each of which preserves its distinctiveness. Pastoral and political activity alike seek to gather in this polyhedron the best of each' (*Evangelii Gaudium*, §236).

With regard to listening to the *sensus fidelium*, the Pope draws two conclusions from this model of the polyhedron: the importance of listening to *everyone* in the Church (all of the facets constitute the polyhedron); and the importance of *diversity* for the health of the Church (all sides are distinct). He goes on to say: 'even people who can be considered dubious on account of their errors have something to offer which must not be overlooked' (*Evangelii Gaudium*, §236). We are a long way here from the axiom often quoted at the Second Vatican Council by those who wanted to condemn atheists, other non-Christian believers, and other Christian believers: 'error has no rights'. Here his concern is attention to 'the whole': 'The Gospel has an intrinsic principle of totality' (*Evangelii Gaudium*, §237). The 'fullness and richness [of the Gospel] embrace scholars and workers, businessmen and artists, in a word, everyone' (*Evangelii Gaudium*, §237). With regard to the second, diversity, here his concern is attention to 'the parts'. If 'the whole is greater than the part, [which] is also greater than the

---

Third Extraordinary General Assembly of the Synod of Bishops, 6 October 2014, available at: https://w2.vatican.va/content/francesco/en/speeches/2014/october/documents/papa-francesco_20141006_padri-sinodali.html.

[10] In Address, 17 October 2015, but quoting his address in St Peter's Square on 4 October 2014, the eve of the first synod, available at: http://w2.vatican.va/content/francesco/en/speeches/2014/october/documents/papa-francesco_20141004_incontro-per-la-famiglia.html.

[11] A polyhedron is a solid body with several flat sides or facets, much like a round diamond or a soccer ball.

sum of its parts', 'there is no need, then, to be overly obsessed with limited and particular questions. We constantly have to broaden our horizons and see the greater good which will benefit us all. But this has to be done without evasion or uprooting' (*Evangelii Gaudium*, §235).

7. Greater Appreciation of 'Provisionality' and the Continuing Guidance of the Holy Spirit

Finally, *WTW*'s proposal of possible receptive learning from Anglicans' promotion of 'open and sometimes painful debate' relates to another Anglican sensibility, a tolerance for 'provisionality' in matters of teaching and governance. That the Roman Catholic Church can learn to be humbler when it teaches the relevance of the Gospel for a particular time and place is one of the more challenging conclusions of ARCIC III's deliberations. In paragraph 148, we find:

> *The authority structures of the Anglican Communion make much more modest claims than do parallel Roman Catholic instruments. As a consequence, Anglicans live with judgements that are understood to be more provisional, requiring to be tested and discerned by the sensus fidelium.*
>
> *Christians are confronted with new situations in evolving history. They have to discern whether new ways of life are in agreement with the Gospel. The sensus fidelium plays an indispensable role in this process of discernment. It takes time before the Church comes to a final judgement. The faithful at large, theologians, and bishops all have their respective roles to play. This requires that Catholics live with provisionality, and give latitude to those instruments which cannot give judgements of the highest authority. By learning to live with teaching that is improvable, space would be given to the testing and discernment of a proposed teaching.*

Echoes of this notion of provisionality can be heard in the teachings of Pope Francis. In his *Evangelii Gaudium* (§§222–25), he speaks of an important principle: 'time is greater than space'. 'This principle enables us to work slowly but surely, without being obsessed with immediate results. It helps us patiently to endure difficult and adverse situations, or inevitable changes in our plans. It invites us to accept the tension between fullness and limitation, and to give a priority to time' (*Evangelii Gaudium*, §223). The Pope goes on to speak of 'attention to the bigger picture, openness to suitable processes and concern for the long run. The Lord himself, during his earthly life, often warned his disciples that there were things they could not yet understand and that they would have to await the Holy Spirit' (*Evangelii Gaudium*, §225).

Time can open up new perspectives on issues, or rather: over time, God can reveal to human beings new perspectives on the meaning of the Gospel. As Pope Francis himself stated, 'It is not enough to find a new language in which to articulate our perennial faith; it is also urgent, in the light of the new challenges and prospects facing humanity, that the Church be able to express the "new things" of Christ's Gospel, that, albeit present in the word of God, have not yet come to light. This is the treasury of "things old and new" of which Jesus spoke when he invited his disciples to teach the newness that he had brought, without forsaking the old (cf. Mt 13:52).'[12]

These seven possibilities for Catholic learning are provocative challenges emerging from an ecumenical dialogue that offers them out of fraternal care. They are now gifts to be received.

Conclusion

By foregrounding the tensions and difficulties that Catholics experience regarding 'instruments of communion' at the local, regional, and universal levels, and by highlighting the gifts that Anglicans might just provide from its strengths in precisely those areas, *WTW* has demonstrated the value of receptive ecumenism. *WTW*, through putting this methodology into practice, has provided the space where each tradition can ask the question of itself: where at the local, regional, and universal levels of church life are we experiencing tensions and difficulties, and what can the other, in fraternal care, offer to help us? Whereas previous ecumenical methodologies may have found differences between the traditions as the problem to be solved, receptive ecumenism sees opportunity in these very differences. As *WTW* puts it: 'The aim here is not to eradicate these differences. The point rather is to ask how each might be a resource for the other so that what is experienced as grace and benefit in one might help address what is less developed in the other' (§46). Therefore, *WTW* has admirably demonstrated the advantages of the receptive ecumenism approach.

One final, albeit minor, point could be made. Surprisingly, *WTW* fails to draw on one source that supports why it should now receive a positive official response within the Roman Catholic Church. This source is Pope John Paul II's apostolic letter *Novo Millennio Ineunte*. From a Roman Catholic perspective, this important papal document could well have

---

[12] Address on the Anniversary of the Catechism of the Catholic Church, 11 October 2017, available at: http://www.pcpne.va/content/pcpne/en/news/2017-10-12-vaticanradio.html.

provided solid backing for its receptive ecumenism methodology and its golden thread, communion ecclesiology. In support of the former, it might well have quoted Pope John Paul II's statement: 'A spirituality of communion implies also the ability to see what is positive in others, to welcome it and prize it as a gift from God: not only as a gift for the brother or sister who has received it directly, but also as a "gift for me"' (*Novo Millennio Ineunte*, §43). In support of the latter, John Paul II stated, in calling for a *development* of the Second Vatican Council's communion ecclesiology: 'the new century will have to see us more than ever intent on valuing *and developing* the forums and structures which, in accordance with the Second Vatican Council's major directives, serve to ensure and safeguard communion' (*Novo Millennio Ineunte*, §44). Tellingly, in the next paragraph (§45), the Pope then goes on to speak of the need to safeguard and promote communion at all levels of the Church:

> *Communion must be cultivated and extended day by day and at every level in the structures of each [local] Church's life. There, relations between Bishops, priests and deacons, between Pastors and the entire People of God, between clergy and Religious, between associations and ecclesial movements must all be clearly characterized by communion. To this end, the structures of participation envisaged by Canon Law, such as the Council of Priests and the Pastoral Council, must be ever more highly valued. These of course are not governed by the rules of parliamentary democracy, because they are consultative rather than deliberative; yet this does not mean that they are less meaningful and relevant. The theology and spirituality of communion encourage a fruitful dialogue between Pastors and faithful: on the one hand uniting them a priori in all that is essential, and on the other leading them to pondered agreement in matters open to discussion. To this end, we need to make our own the ancient pastoral wisdom which, without prejudice to their authority, encouraged Pastors to listen more widely to the entire People of God.*

John Paul II then quotes two exemplars of the tradition regarding this principle of encouraging participation by all and listening to all. Firstly, St Benedict in his Rule wrote: 'By the Lord's inspiration, it is often a younger person who knows what is best.'[13] Secondly, St Paulinus of Nola 'urges': 'Let us listen to what all the faithful say, because in every one of them the Spirit of God breathes.'[14]

---

[13] 'Ideo autem omnes ad consilium vocari diximus, quia saepe iuniori Dominus revelat quod melius est.' *Regula*, III, 3.

[14] 'De omnium fidelium ore pendeamus, quia in omnem fidelem Spiritus Dei spirat.' *Epistola* 23, 36 to Sulpicius Severus, *CSEL* 29, 193.

In conclusion, there are many parallels between the receptive learning possibilities for the Roman Catholic Church proposed by *WTW* and Pope Francis's vision for renewal and reform according to the Second Vatican Council. In other words, the Anglican tradition has much to offer in making the Council a reality. Paradoxically, then, the Anglican tradition can assist the Roman Catholic Church to be more faithful to the vision of the Second Vatican Council.

Bibliography

ARCIC II, *The Gift of Authority (Authority in the Church III)* (1999), available at: www.vatican.va/roman_curia/pontifical_councils/chrstuni/documents/rc_pc_chrstuni_doc_12051999_gift-of-autority_en.html.

Ekpo, Anthony, *The Breath of the Spirit in the Church: Sensus Fidelium and Canon Law* (Strathfield: St Pauls Publications, 2014).

Extraordinary Synod of Bishops, *Final Report* (1985), available at: www.vatican.va/roman_curia/synod/documents/rc_synod_doc_20151026_relazione-finale-xiv-assemblea_en.html.

Kasper, Walter, 'The Church as Communion: Reflections on the Guiding Ecclesiological Idea of the Second Vatican Council', in *Theology and Church* (New York: Crossroad, 1989), pp. 148–65.

Pope Francis, Address on the Anniversary of the Catechism of the Catholic Church, 11 October 2017, available at: http://www.pcpne.va/content/pcpne/en/news/2017-10-12-vaticanradio.html.

Pope Francis, Address Commemorating the 50th Anniversary of the Institution of the Synod of Bishops, 17 October 2015, available at: http://w2.vatican.va/content/francesco/en/speeches/2015/october/documents/papa-francesco_20151017_50-anniversario-sinodo.html.

Pope Francis, *Misericordiae Vultus* (11 April 2015), available at: https://w2.vatican.va/content/francesco/en/apost_letters/documents/papa-francesco_bolla_20150411_misericordiae-vultus.html.

Pope Francis, Greeting to the Synod Fathers during the First General Congregation of the Third Extraordinary General Assembly of the Synod of Bishops, 6 October 2014, available at: https://w2.vatican.va/content/francesco/en/speeches/2014/october/documents/papa-francesco_20141006_padri-sinodali.html.

Pope Francis, Address in St Peter's Square, 4 October 2014, available at: http://w2.vatican.va/content/francesco/en/speeches/2014/october/documents/papa-francesco_20141004_incontro-per-la-famiglia.html.

Pope Francis, *Evangelii Gaudium*. Apostolic Exhortation on the Proclamation of the Gospel in Today's World (24 November 2013), available at: http://w2.vatican.va/content/francesco/en/apost_exhortations/documents/papa-francesco_esortazione-ap_20131124_evangelii-gaudium.html.

Pope Francis and His Grace Justin Welby, Archbishop of Canterbury, 'Common Declaration' (5 October 2016), available at: www.anglicannews.org/news/2016/10/common-declaration-of-pope-francis-and-archbishop-justin-welby.aspx and www.vatican.va/roman_curia/pontifical_councils/chrstuni/angl-comm-docs/rc_pc_chrstuni_doc_20161005_dichiarazione-comune_en.html.

Pope John Paul II, *Novo Millennio Ineunte* (6 January 2001), available at:

http://w2.vatican.va/content/john-paul-ii/en/apost_letters/2001/documents/ hf_jp-ii_apl_20010106_novo-millennio-ineunte.html.

Pope Paul VI, 'Closing Address: Fourth Session', in *Council Daybook: Vatican II, Session 4,* ed. Floyd Anderson (Washington, DC: National Catholic Welfare Conference, 1966), pp. 359–62.

Pope Paul VI, *Gaudium et Spes* (7 December 1965), available at: www.vatican. va/archive/hist_councils/ii_vatican_council/documents/vat-ii_cons_ 19651207_gaudium-et-spes_en.html.

Ratzinger, Cardinal Joseph, 'Ecumenismo: crisis o svolta? Dialogo tra il Card. J. Ratzinger e il teologo protestante P. Ricca', *Nuova Umanità,* 15 (1993) 101–21, available at https://www.cittanuova.it/cn-download/10730/10731.

Second Vatican Council, *Lumen Gentium.* The Dogmatic Constitution on the Church (21 November 1964), available at: www.vatican.va/archive/hist_councils/ii_ vatican_council/documents/vat-ii_const_19641121_lumen-gentium_en.html.

Second Vatican Council, *Unitatis Redintegratio.* Decree on Ecumenism (21 November 1964), available at: www.vatican.va/archive/hist_councils/ii_vatican_council/ documents/vat-ii_decree_19641121_unitatis-redintegratio_en.html.

Walking Together on the Way: Learning to Be the Church— Local, Regional, Universal

An Anglican Commentary
James Hawkey

An Anglican Commentary on *Walking Together on the Way: Learning to Be the Church—Local, Regional, Universal* of the Anglican–Roman Catholic International Commission

James Hawkey, Dean of Clare College, Cambridge

Preface

Walking Together on the Way: Learning to Be the Church—Local, Regional, Universal (henceforth, *WTW*), the first Agreed Statement of the third round of the Anglican–Roman Catholic International Commission (ARCIC III), consciously builds on the high level of doctrinal consensus and real-but-imperfect communion which already exists between the Roman Catholic Church and the Anglican Communion. It responds to the challenge laid out in the 2006 Common Declaration of Pope Benedict XVI and Archbishop Rowan Williams to examine the fundamental nature of the Church as Communion,[1] and within that reality to explore how ethical teaching might be discerned in both the local and the universal Church. From the beginning of the Co-Chairs' Preface, this document is identified as the first part of that very major project.

From its inception, the ARCIC process has sought to explore theological issues in a way which seeks to approach contested questions from fresh, shared perspectives. Well beyond historical caricature and the polemic of the past, two previous ARCIC phases have produced a series of diverse reports (listed in full in §2) which express a remarkable level of agreement on many matters once considered Church-dividing. In 1980, Pope John Paul II praised the ARCIC methodology, as going 'behind the habit of thought and expression born and nourished in enmity and controversy, to scrutinize together the great common treasure, to clothe it in a language at once traditional and expressive of the insights of an age which no longer glories in strife but seeks to come together in listening to the quiet voice of the Spirit'.[2] The ARCIC process and its statements are extraordinary fruits of the Spirit, compelling Anglicans and Roman Catholics towards deeper communion in Christ.

This document takes us a step further. The title itself speaks of the whole Church *in via*—not as a perfect society, but in language familiar to both communions as a pilgrim people. The metaphor of a joint pilgrimage is a

---

1 Pope Benedict XVI and the Archbishop of Canterbury, His Grace Rowan Williams, 'Common Declaration' (23 November 2006), available at: http://w2.vatican.va/content/benedict-xvi/en/speeches/2006/november/documents/hf_ben-xvi_spe_20061123_common-decl.html.
2 Address of John Paul II to ARCIC I, Castelgandolfo, 4 September 1980, available at: https://w2.vatican.va/content/john-paul-ii/en/speeches/1980/september/documents/hf_jp-ii_spe_19800904_cattolici-anglicani.html.

dynamic and pastoral one. It has profound implications for much of what we say about one another and how we say it. As the Co-Chairs put it, this is a task of conversion and renewal for both partners, not a simple return to unity or uniformity, but rather an organic growth into 'the fullness of communion in Christ and the Spirit'. The remaining questions of ethics—how to live—and authority—how to live *together*—should be seen in this context.

Anyone who has ever made a pilgrimage in the company of others knows how belongings sometimes get mixed up on the journey. Indeed, what was considered private property at the outset often becomes communal by the end. The exchange of theological gifts which has characterized ARCIC's rich theological dialogue since 1970 has been mirrored by a sharing of symbolic gifts. Most famously, the newly refreshed relationship between our churches is rooted in the gift of Pope Paul VI's episcopal ring to Archbishop Michael Ramsey in Rome in March 1966. On one level, this recognition of a form of apostolic ministry by Pope Paul imaged the Second Vatican Council's commitment to the 'special place'[3] occupied by the Anglican Communion. Others have compared this gesture to the sign of a betrothal. Other gifts followed over the subsequent years, including pectoral crosses to bishops and stoles to clergy. Most recently, on 5 October 2016, at the church of San Gregorio al Celio in Rome, the very site from which Pope St Gregory the Great sent St Augustine to England, Pope Francis presented Archbishop Welby with a replica of a pastoral staff which had, by tradition, belonged to St Gregory. Very movingly Archbishop Welby then carried this crosier at an ecumenical Evening Prayer alongside the Cardinal Secretary of State the following evening. After Pope Francis had given Archbishop Welby the crosier, the Archbishop employed a symbolic gesture of his own, removing his own pectoral Cross of Nails[4] and giving it to Pope Francis. Commissioning nineteen pairs of Anglican and Roman Catholic bishops from the International Anglican–Roman Catholic Commission for Unity and Mission (IARCCUM) for joint mission in their own contexts, fifty

---

[3] Decree on Ecumenism *Unitatis Redintegratio* §13, in *Vatican Council II: Constitutions, Decrees, Declarations*, ed. Austin Flannery OP (New York: Costello, 2007), p. 513.

[4] The Coventry Cross of Nails is made from three nails from the roof of the bombed cathedral. It has become an international symbol of peace and reconciliation. Today's Community of the Cross of Nails is a network of individuals and institutions inspired by the story of Coventry's destruction and renewal, committed to reconciliation. Reconciliation is one of the three priority areas for Archbishop Welby's ministry, alongside prayer and the religious life, and evangelism and witness.

years after that first historic meeting, Pope and Archbishop stood along-side one another as ministers of reconciliation within and between their communions. As a symbol of joint ministry in the contemporary world, these IARCCUM bishops were each given a Lampedusa Cross by Pope and Archbishop, fashioned out of the timbers of wrecked boats which had once carried refugees across the dangers of the Mediterranean Sea. This weighty language of symbols needs to be read and understood alongside the ARCIC process as a profound counterpoint, underpinning, explaining, and developing the pilgrim journey of communion. There have been symbolic visits as well as gifts—each Archbishop of Canterbury since Geoffrey Fisher has visited the Pope (often frequently), cardinals have attended Lambeth Conferences, and Anglican bishops have sometimes accompanied their Roman Catholic counterparts on *ad limina* visits to Rome, something which many hope will become a normal feature of such occasions, which was recommended in *The Gift of Authority* (1999) and is recalled in *WTW* (§147). When Pope John Paul II visited Canterbury in 1982, he prayed alongside Archbishop Runcie at Canterbury Cathedral, the Mother Church of the Anglican Communion, and during his State Visit to the United Kingdom in September 2010 Pope Benedict co-presided at Evening Prayer in Westminster Abbey with Archbishop Williams. The two prelates prayed alongside one another in the Shrine of St Edward the Confessor, and jointly gave the blessing at the conclusion of the liturgy, having also addressed a joint gathering of Anglican and Roman Catholic bishops earlier that day.

It would be a profound mistake to see this document—different in character and style from the rest of the ARCIC corpus—as a step back from the goal of full ecclesial communion. *WTW* is honest about remaining areas of difference between our two communions, some important, some surely adiaphora. But this pilgrimage is not a wandering perambulation. Rather it is, as the full title suggests, a journey 'on the Way' to full communion. The early Christian communities were frequently themselves described as *tes odou*—the Way—probably through association with John 14.6, where Jesus describes himself as such. We recognize this 'Way' in one another, as Christians together, seeking deeper unity through a deeper implication in Christ, and expecting to receive gifts from one another's traditions.

WTW illustrates how the cultural, social, and structural challenges of living together in Christ are shared challenges in which our churches can learn from one another. The methodology of the document is profoundly shaped by the insights of receptive ecumenism, pioneered and developed by Professor Paul Murray (a Roman Catholic member of the Commission), and initially unfolded at a conference in Durham in January 2006. Very simply, this method does not allow for the ecclesial self-sufficiency of any church, and contributes towards our deeper reception of a communion theology. The first question for one Christian partner approaching another in dialogue is not 'What can the other learn from us?', but rather 'What can we learn or receive from the other?'[5] At a Bible study at the first receptive ecumenism conference, Philip Endean reflected, 'The *communio* of the Church, its unity in diversity is not something complete ... Rather God's subversive touch is always opening that communion more widely.'[6] Dialogue is itself a means of reconciling grace, and of discovering what fresh gifts the Holy Spirit has in store for each to receive from the other.

Since the sixteenth century, Anglicanism has frequently made use of this kind of receptive learning, borrowing from other traditions and integrating such borrowings into its own life. That is the way of things in a church which is profoundly shaped by the cultures in which she is set, and which is consciously both Catholic and Reformed. In their Preface to *WTW*, the Co-Chairs remark that the final meeting of the Commission was in Erfurt, where Martin Luther was ordained. Primarily for reasons rooted in British politics,[7] Luther was not quite as influential on early Anglicanism as his French contemporary Jean Calvin. But in his profoundly influential book *The Gospel and the Catholic Church*, Archbishop Michael Ramsey claimed that the whole Church—Catholicism—'always stands before the door of Wittenburg to read the truth by which she is created and by which also she is judged'.[8] Both in the pontificate of Pope Francis and in the contemporary Anglican Communion, we see much evidence of the outworking of such a reforming dynamic in the Church's life. For us as fellow pilgrims, the profound truth of grace as limitless, transformative, free gift is one which the whole Church is summoned to learn again and again. *WTW* reminds us that we see such grace in the other, and it prompts us to ensure that our mutual learning is as graceful as the gift we ultimately long to receive. The hope of ARCIC III is that this

---

[5] For a full exposition of the receptive ecumenism method and rationale, see Paul D. Murray (ed.), *Receptive Ecumenism and the Call to Catholic Learning* (Oxford: Oxford University Press, 2008).

[6] Philip Endean SJ, 'Prologue to Part One', in Murray (ed.), *Receptive Ecumenism*, p. 3.

[7] Henry VIII engaged in detailed theological controversy with Luther. He responded to Luther's attack on the Catholic Church in *De Captivitate Babylonica* ('On the Babylonian Captivity') with his own *Assertio Septem Sacramentorum* ('Defence of the Seven Sacraments'). Henry was rewarded for his opposition to Luther by Pope Leo X with the title *Fidei Defensor* (still used by British sovereigns today).

[8] Michael Ramsey, *The Gospel and the Catholic Church* (London: Longman, 1936), p. 180.

Agreed Statement will not live in a bilateral vacuum, but might contribute towards the wider ecumenical journey. As with the great Lutheran–Roman Catholic bilateral *Joint Declaration on the Doctrine of Justification*, this document and its methodology are to be celebrated and received by a wider ecumenical audience, inspiring a joyful humility on the part of each communion in learning from the other, and inspiring greater confidence in Christ who calls us to encounter him and one another in the refashioning depths of paschal communion.

This commentary will now proceed following the structure of the Agreed Statement itself.

I. Introduction

Right from the start, as the document gives the reader an overview of what has been achieved so far (§§1–4, 15–16), the final goal of the dialogue is made explicit. That gift, which we receive together from the heart of the Trinity, is nothing less than full visible unity. The last couple of decades have frequently been described as an 'Ecumenical Winter', but this Introduction details the work completed by the Commission since 1971 and reveals significant convergence on the essentials of shared faith and life.

The 'gift exchange' is a frequently used metaphor in ecumenical dialogue,[1] helping us to understand both the need for receptivity to one another and the profound theological truth that Christian unity is primarily a gift to be received from God, in Christ and through the power of the Holy Spirit for the whole Church.[2] Thus, we participate in receiving that gift, and mediate it to one another. We never build the unity of the Church in our own strength.

One of the most profound developments in ecumenical theology over the last twenty years has been a move from the language of 'unity' to the more dynamic language of 'communion'. Previous ARCIC documents, notably *Church as Communion* (1991), *Life in Christ* (1994), and *The Gift of Authority* (1999), have contributed to this move, and have helped to reframe broader ecumenical conversation. While the documents of ARCIC II have not been formally 'received' by a Lambeth Conference, ARCIC I's ground-breaking work on eucharistic doctrine, ministry, and ordination was judged by Lambeth 1988 as 'consonant in substance with the faith of Anglicans'.[3] The response from Anglican provinces to the 1976 and 1981 work on authority was generally warm, although many requested further work on primacy, collegiality, and the role of the laity. This challenge was answered by ARCIC II with work on primacy and collegiality, and arguably *WTW* opens the door to a much deeper theological reflection on the role of the laity in the life of both communions while admitting that there is very much more to be learned.

WTW is honest and realistic about matters which remain communion-dividing. There is still 'distance to be travelled' (§5). But the context of

---

[1] This mechanism is described as part of the inner-dynamic of the Church in *Lumen Gentium* §13 (see *Vatican Council II*, ed. Flannery, p. 17).

[2] *WTW* §13 for a short unpacking of this theology of gift in the ARCIC context.

[3] Lambeth 1988, resolution 8.1, in *The Lambeth Conference: Resolutions Archive from 1988*, available at: www.anglicancommunion.org/media/127749/1988.pdf.

1

that remaining pilgrimage is one of what has sometimes been described as 'money in the bank'.[4] New issues which have arisen, not necessarily anticipated during those hopeful early years of the ARCIC process, such as the inclusion of women in the three orders of ministry in many provinces of the Anglican Communion and the development of conversations surrounding sexuality and gender, have posed new challenges. The document is keen to point out that these issues not only are not problematic in themselves, but also highlight questions of authority. For Roman Catholics and others, it is perhaps hard to see how one communion can contain such diversity of practice, while for many Anglicans, provincial authority and a developed sense of adiaphora are sufficient to justify such difference.

However, the Anglican Communion is hardly blind to the many questions its own practice highlights. *The Virginia Report*,[5] *The Windsor Report*,[6] and the process surrounding a potential Anglican Communion Covenant are all responses to dealing with the ongoing question of the limits of diversity within a communion ecclesiology. How theological developments are 'received' *within* a church is as important a question as how they are received *between* churches. Some of the challenges of different views between and within churches might be characterized as more cultural than theological. But we should perhaps resist coming to one or other conclusion too swiftly, as issues of theology and culture are so frequently knotted together.

WTW's honesty about the remaining areas of difference between Anglicans and Roman Catholics is matched by its honesty about similarity and difference in our churches' historic and cultural experience. We live together in a globalized age, sharing a mixed inheritance of colonialism and expansion, and exposure to radically different particular cultures which impact in diverse and complex ways. 'Given this new global context', the document says, 'the tasks of engaging with cultures, religions, and stark social inequalities take new forms. Anglicans and Catholics alike need to develop local and trans-local structures which enable them

---

[4] 'ARCIC—Dead in the Water or Money in the Bank?' was the title of Cardinal Cormac Murphy-O'Connor's Richard Stewart Lecture at Worth Abbey in 2009. The full text can be found at: www.catholicnews.org.uk/Home/News/2009/Cardinal-Cormac-Murphy-O-Connor-delivers-lecture-on-ecumenism.

[5] Inter-Anglican Theological and Doctrinal Commission, *The Virginia Report* (London: Anglican Consultative Council, 1997), available at: www.anglicancommunion.org/media/150889/report-1.pdf.

[6] Lambeth Commission on Communion, *The Windsor Report* (London: The Anglican Communion Office, 2004), available at: www.anglicancommunion.org/media/68225/windsor2004full.pdf.

to draw closer to one another as they engage with the challenges of a new age' (§7). The point is that neither of our communions can simply rely on traditional models or ways of dealing with newly arising cultural issues. Neither of our churches can claim that everything can be neatly sorted out. The challenge which *WTW* begins to present is how we can learn from one another on the way as we commit together to deeper Christian faithfulness.

All of this leads into the real heart of ARCIC III's work so far. How can we, within such a context, articulate the relationship between the local churches and the universal Church, and thus come to some conclusions about how authoritative teaching might work? Alongside the traditional two ecclesiological categories of local and universal, *WTW* introduces the very helpful third category of the regional: groupings of local churches confined to particular geographic areas. A focus on the regional opens up an interesting set of coordinates for the Church as the space in which the local and universal really meet. Some consideration of this theme has already occurred in other dialogues,[7] but *WTW* is extremely helpful for gaining a theological sense of the value and symbolism of the 'trans-local'—defined in the document glossary as 'any expression of church life beyond the level of the diocese'—beyond its usefulness for straightforward sociological analysis. Do regional bodies have an ecclesiological value beyond that of utility? What weight ought to be given to local synods, to their consideration of controversy and development? Might controlled, localized controversy have a great value for the universal in helping to discern, for example, whether a new development might ultimately be received by the whole Church?

There is a remarkable statement—a significant achievement—in paragraph 12 that 'Dialogue within our respective traditions about such difficult matters as the proper place for decisions on questions of ministry and human sexuality should be welcomed rather than feared.' For Anglicans, this is an encouraging and timely evaluation of our internal situation which reminds us that theological discernment can never be a zero-sum game. It is also perhaps a fruit of a Jesuit papacy, in which Pope Francis is encouraging all Christians to speak openly and honestly. Beginning from a situation of fragmentation '*between* our traditions and ... *within* them' (§13), the document offers a road map for the second part of the mandate, which is to consider precisely how ethical discernment

---

[7] For example, *WTW* notes the 2007 Ravenna Statement of the Roman Catholic–Orthodox dialogue.

can occur. *WTW*'s insistent point is that such discernment will be strongest when it is pursued together, because the life of the Church is a dynamic expression of and sharing in communion. To allow for this kind of deep discernment, our structures need to be evaluated to ensure that they are maximally able to serve such work.

The *Windsor Report* of 2004 introduced the concept of adiaphora to contemporary Anglican theological reflection. Simply, there are some issues of diversity which should not be considered communion-dividing. As the *Windsor Report* puts it, 'Anglicans have always recognised a key distinction between core doctrines of the church ... and those upon which disagreement can be tolerated without endangering unity.'[8] However, the Anglican Communion is not alone in being far from clear in discerning what might and what might not be considered adiaphora, and how far the concept might be stretched. In his 2009 Willebrands Lecture in Rome, Archbishop Rowan Williams developed this notion in the arena of Anglican/Roman Catholic discernment by posing important and challenging questions in the context of ARCIC's 'money in the bank'. Dr Williams said, '... the major question that remains is whether in the light of that depth of agreement the issues that still divide us have the same weight ... When so very much agreement has been firmly established in first-order matters about the identity and mission of the Church, is it really justifiable to treat other issues as equally vital for its health and integrity?'[9] *WTW* asks whether divisive issues should be revisited if ecumenical engagement is rooted in 'explicit ecclesial self-critique' (§14). Such receptive learning has the capacity to remove the sting from the way we evaluate one another as Christian communities. It is a cry for grace, because it first recognizes our own incompleteness. That is the context for the 're-reception' (§16) of the deep truths of the faith, and of the fresh insight into that truth which the Holy Spirit always offers the whole Church.

At the end of the Introduction (§21), we are presented with a distilled theological methodology which underpins the receptive ecumenical process. Put simply: Christian churches live alongside one another in similar cultural contexts all over the world. Every context will throw up particular challenges which demand careful discernment so that the Church may be faithful to God and to God's people. This discernment is not always straightforward, and our different theological traditions and

---

[8] Lambeth Commission on Communion, *The Windsor Report*, sect. A, §36.
[9] Rowan Williams, Willebrands Lecture, Rome, 2009, available at: http://aoc2013.brix.fatbee-hive.com/articles.php/766/archbishops-address-at-a-willebrands-symposium-in-rome

ecclesial structures may not always allow for unified, simple answers. However, the Anglican–Roman Catholic pilgrimage, underpinned by a very high level of agreement on the fundamentals of the faith, is an intensification of unity despite difference. The communion we already share and which is increasing by degrees is robust enough to deal with this. That is itself a powerful witness. Such communion—*koinonia*—is always evangelistic, reaching beyond itself, but it is also didactic in a broader sense, showing a fractured and fracturing world how unity in diversity can be modelled. It is the vocation of both our churches to now unpack and interrogate the implications of these insights.

II. The Church Local and Universal in the Apostolic and Post-Apostolic Periods

The initial formal divisions of the English Reformation were structural. They also included tensions between contrasting views of the relationship between the local and universal Church. During the Henrician period (1509–47), structural and canonical changes in England preceded wider formal doctrinal and liturgical reform. However, more than four centuries of separated ecclesial life have led to diversity in structures which both reflects and creates differing patterns of authority and governance. Before moving into analysis of how these patterns have settled into recognizable and describable contours in our contemporary communions, *WTW* has a brief exploration of the diversity of Christian life in its earliest years.

Paul Minear's seminal work *Images of the Church in the New Testament*, first published in 1960, offers ninety-six images of the Church from the pages of Christian Scripture.[10] *WTW* chooses to focus almost solely on one—*ekklesia*—to unpack what the New Testament means when it speaks of the gathered Christian community. This word is often used interchangeably to describe local or individual Christian communities as well as for the increasingly dispersed communities of Christians which make up the whole body of Christ. This simple fact helps to underpin the document's conclusion in paragraph 31, reminiscent of other ecumenical agreements, that 'Each local church that is in communion with other local churches is the Church of God in that place.'

WTW has a rich theology of the Church, illustrated in this section by reference to Scripture, and building on substantial agreement in other

---

10 Paul Minear, *Images of the Church in the New Testament* (Philadelphia: Westminster, 1960), p. 24.

phases of the ARCIC dialogue, which often relies on diverse scriptural images. The Church's mission, rooted in Jesus' own command to make disciples of all nations, is international and inter-cultural. Christian disciples are to reach out to all in the knowledge that Christ's saving and sanctifying grace is for all people, who should be gathered into the community which is Christ's body.

Much is made in the early part of this section of the role of Jerusalem and its Church (see §§25, 32, 33, 35, 37). As well as being the locus of Jesus' passion and resurrection, Jerusalem has a broader, dynamic typological resonance in the Bible. Not only was it the heart of Jewish worship, but it was also seen as the ultimate pilgrim destination, and the sacred site which would gather all people in the last days. Jerusalem is often portrayed (especially, for example, in Psalm 87) as a mother, generating as well as gathering children. Jerusalem is a place for all places, in a way not dissimilar to how the Church understands Jesus as a human for all humans:[11]Jerusalem is a priestly city, and a priestly church, which has a strong eschatological dynamism, as *WTW* points out, even after its destruction in AD 70 (§37). The book of Revelation, with its visions addressed to particular churches—Ephesus, Smyrna, Pergamum, and so on—culminates in a vibrant vision of the New Jerusalem, with its gates continually open (Rev 21.25), so that all who worship the Lamb may enter. Each of these particular churches has an angel,[12] to whom a message is delivered by the seer. In Patristic tradition these angels are often described as bishops, a theme developed in much Anglican commentary and preaching of the seventeenth century. There are clear scriptural building blocks here for later reflection on communion between bishops, who are depicted as representing their churches.

Rome also features significantly in this section. It was the centre of the ancient world and of the imperial cult, and the preaching of St Paul right at Rome's heart in the Acts of the Apostles is St Luke's final statement of the universality of the Gospel. The change in emphasis from the authority of the Jerusalem church to that of Rome was an important development during the post-Apostolic period, and one which would benefit from further elucidation. How and why Rome became the arbiter of orthodoxy, with traditions developing around the martyrdoms of Peter and Paul, the

---

[11] Gregory of Nazianzus famously wrote in his Epistle 101, a critique of Apollinarius, 'For that which he has not assumed, he has not healed.' This is a central tenet of Christian teaching about the Incarnation of Christ.

[12] In Revelation, the seer is commissioned to communicate with the 'angels' of particular churches.

increasing dominance of the mission to the gentiles, changes in the Roman Empire, and the wide geographical spread of the Christian faith by the end of the second century, is a complex story. For Anglicans, further reflection on the relationship between Jerusalem and Rome could raise interesting questions about communion and the focus of unity. In particular, the emergence of the figure of Peter and his relationship with the other apostles is of great importance. Although Roman Catholics are bound by the dogmatic definitions of universal jurisdiction and infallibility, Pope John Paul II's remarkable plea in *Ut Unum Sint* of 1995 for 'patient and fraternal dialogue' with ecumenical partners on the role and nature of the papacy is an essential encouragement in considering church structures.[13] Classical Anglican texts of the late sixteenth and early seventeenth centuries make a characteristic point that they object not to the authority given to Peter as Bishop of Rome per se, but rather to the privileging of Peter (as they see it) beyond the wider episcopal college. This is rooted in scriptural critique: many Anglicans would argue that Peter's *faith* is the rock on which the Church is built, and that the Petrine commission of Matthew 16 needs to be balanced with the wider scriptural witness and the commissioning of the whole apostolic college.

From paragraph 29 onwards, the document builds from Scripture the ecclesial categories of local, trans-local, and universal, pointing to diversity within the local, but also to a unity of faith, behaviour, and purpose within the universal. Scripture and the earliest traditions show that churches such as those of Jerusalem and Antioch generate other families of churches (§30), such that early 'instruments of communion' emerge. This notion of families of churches is perhaps one which should come to the fore as our communion ecclesiology begins to mature, and is developed later in *WTW* as the Commission reflects on how national or regional churches might find a clearer voice.

The document's work on decision-making and the maintenance of communion necessarily compresses a lot of complex detail into several paragraphs. While the history of the early Church is one of the maintenance

---

[13] Pope John Paul II, *Ut Unum Sint*, Encyclical on Commitment to Ecumenism (1995), §96, available at: http://w2.vatican.va/content/john-paul-ii/en/encyclicals/documents/hf_jp-ii_ enc_25051995_ut-unum-sint.html. The Church of England's response to *Ut Unum Sint*, *May They All Be One'*, House of Bishops Occasional Paper (London: Church House Publishing, 1997), highlights the need to look afresh at the structures of the first millennium of Christianity, and also to examine the current needs of the Church to discern what kind of universal primacy might be needed for unity, and how it might be exercised in relation to other structures in the Church.

of communion, it is also one which interrogates and tests the robustness of that communion. The famous disagreement between Peter and Paul at Antioch recorded in Galatians 2 perhaps deserves a little more focus in the overall context of this section. It is hard for contemporary Christians to understand the sheer weight of the issues at stake here,[14] and the precariousness of the early Church's mission as a result. There is conflict and disagreement right at the heart of the earliest Christian witness over matters which were regarded as 'Church-dividing'. Most modern editions of the New Testament end Paul's speech to Peter in Galatians 2 at verse 14. However, New Testament Greek does not include speech-marks, and many commentators think that Paul's speech concludes at the end of Galatians 2. If so, Paul's angry rhetorical outburst to Peter, in which he accuses him of promoting justification through the Law, 'Then Christ died for nothing', represents a threat to the fabric of Christian communion if ever there was one.

Similarly, the document helpfully refers to the problem of eating idol meat recorded in 1 Corinthians (§36), where those who are 'strong' are urged to check their own practice for the sake of the 'weak'. Some Anglicans have drawn an analogy between this situation and the principle of 'gracious restraint' urged in the drafts of an Anglican Communion Covenant, and in the letter of the Anglican Primates from their 2009 meeting in Alexandria.[15] The final paragraph of this Primates' letter places the call to such gracious restraint alongside that of deeper communion.

More detailed work on the diversity of Church life in the apostolic and post-apostolic periods might be helpful for the ongoing dialogue. In particular, it could be particularly fruitful to reflect on the Johannine voice, particularly in the Johannine letters, where clear comparison is made between the love revealed in the nature of God and the ideal relational model of the Church.

Themes of conciliarity and synodality emerge towards the end of this section, properly alongside reflection on the role of the bishop and the

---

[14] This is a key moment in Christian origins, as the earliest Church moves away from an exclusive Jewish matrix and the demands of that context regarding circumcision and certain dietary restrictions. A so-called 'two-missions' hypothesis, initially proposed by F. C. Baur in the mid-nineteenth century, received its fullest and clearest exposition in Michael Goulder's *A Tale of Two Missions* (Louisville: Westminster John Knox Press, 1994). This binary is not accepted by most Scripture scholars today, but the general thesis is helpful in giving a sense of complex diversity within the earliest Christian communities.

[15] Primates of the Anglican Communion, *Deeper Communion; Gracious Restraint: A Letter from Alexandria to the Churches of the Anglican Communion*, available at: http://anglicancommunion.org/media/68372/Pastoral-Letter.pdf.

primacy of the Bishop of Rome. At this point in the document, the emergence of the monarchical episcopate is slightly assumed without comment, and although the emergent pattern of bishops in communion is not in any doubt, a reference to how *episkope* was modelled in different ways before a settled, normative structure emerged would be a helpful strengthening of other bilateral reflection on the nature of episcopacy.

This section prepares the ground for the sections which are to come. It reflects on a 'pluralist model of witness and authority' (§45), the rootedness of the early Church in relationship with the risen and ascended Christ, guaranteed through the Church's apostolicity, and the experience of robust disagreement within Christian *koinonia*. Using the scriptural witness, it portrays communities which are recognizable to one another in faith and love, because they preach the same Gospel. Two millennia on, our divisions have themselves become structured and formalized. The deep scriptural well is one we need to drink from together, as we recognize one another in its pages.

III. Ecclesial Communion in Christ: The Need for Effective Instruments of Communion

This section is in three subsections. First, paragraphs 46–50 introduce the relationship between the local and the trans-local. Second, paragraphs 51–61 offer a beautiful synthesis of agreed teaching on the nature of baptism and the eucharist as the fundamental sacraments of initiation and ecclesial reality. Third, paragraphs 62–79 provide an introduction to different Roman Catholic and Anglican approaches to how the local is related to various levels of the trans-local, and an initial reflection on how such relationships are maintained and curated at various levels in each of our churches.

The first subsection reminds us that baptism is our common and fundamental entrance into the life of grace. Because of this shared rooting in Christ's death and resurrection, which necessarily impels us to 'eschatological communion, anticipated in eucharistic communion' (§46), Christian divisions which emerge from this point must be considered sinful. Church structures, and by inference what we refer to as instruments of communion, have a vocation actively to 'promote life in the fellowship ... of the Holy Spirit' (§46). This is the first glimpse of an extremely helpful assertion which is voiced several times in this section. Instruments of communion, so often conceived as modes of control, are strongly interpreted in *WTW* as instruments 'to serve the unity and the diversity ... of the Church' (§57). The emphasis is not on an enforced regimented uniformity, but rather on shaping a communion of love which is consistently geared towards the wholeness, health, and holiness of an interdependent body. The opening paragraph 46 itself admits that all structures themselves are by definition 'more limited than the life of grace'. What follows is then a sophisticated analysis not primarily of institutions, but rather of relationships.

It is in this context that we begin to consider autonomy and interrelatedness. For Anglicans, the ecclesiology of *WTW* is as helpful for our own internal housekeeping as it is for conversations with ecumenical partners. There are dangers in over-emphasizing both autonomy and centralization. The health of the whole Church is dependent on a creative tension between the two, held together by love and trust. Wider cultural context is important here, and the complexity inherent in contemporary cultural analysis means that it is often challenging to develop convincing general strategies without attention to each particular.

In paragraph 48, the document mentions almost in passing the dangers of 'insufficient critical distance from the prevailing culture'. There may be all sorts of theological assumptions here about what we have learned to call 'the secular' which do not sit comfortably with parts of the Anglican tradition which see wider culture as itself worthy of respectful discernment and analysis. How our two communions assess what is good, beautiful, and prophetic in wider culture will be a question for the next stage of the Commission's work.

The document's focus on how the local and trans-local are related to each other reveals delicate networks of relationship, where connections are well honed and balanced. To expand the biblical image of the Church as body of Christ, precisely because of the necessity of 'local adaptation' (§49) and cultural (as well as theological) diversity, the muscles and sinews which hold us together need to be able to stretch and to be flexible, formed by a hermeneutic of Christian trust. Those committed to mutuality and communion in the Anglican tradition need to curate structures which celebrate adiaphora while being committed to the life of the whole. The 2015 document of the Inter-Anglican Standing Committee on Unity, Faith and Order, *Towards a Symphony of Instruments*, begins to refocus our structures to 'intentionally and prophetically recall the Communion to its purpose in God's Kingdom'.[16] It is such structures which *WTW* now moves on to describe and interrogate.

---

[16] Inter-Anglican Standing Commission on Unity, Faith and Order, *Towards a Symphony of*

Baptized into the communion of saints

This subsection is a remarkable distillation of agreed teaching between our communions from previous rounds of ARCIC and other ecumenical dialogues. Christian existence, from the immersion of baptism onwards, is necessarily and simultaneously local and trans-local, participating in relational networks across time and space (§§51, 55). It is through baptism, where the believer is clothed with Christ, that each disciple shares in the ministry of Christ's *tria munera*—the triple office of Christ as prophet, priest, and king which St Eusebius of Caesarea articulated in the fourth century. Communion with and in Christ thus allows the whole Church to have confidence in her ultimate indefectibility on matters fundamental to the faith. This is allied to what the document calls an 'instinct for the faith' (§53), which Anglicans will recognize, for example, in the great poets as well as in formal doctrinal formularies. Fundamentally, this *sensus fidei fidelium* is not the sole preserve of formal instruments of communion, nor of great synodical gatherings: it is also a mystical reality, implanted within the human heart and nurtured by the Holy Spirit. It is testified to by the charismatic teacher, the contemplative, and even the Holy Fool. The faith is not a static set of precepts, but alive and active (Heb 4.12), proclaimed afresh in every generation through the inspiration of the Holy Spirit. Thus, discernment of the mind of Christ often takes time and must be rooted in prayerful reflection.

The universality, or catholicity, of the Church demands each Christian community's liberation from the idol of self-sufficiency. *WTW* warns of the dangers of local churches turning-in on themselves, recalling Martin Luther's masterful definition of sin as 'incurvatus in se est'.[17] By way of this analogy, we touch on the heart of the document's methodology: each church must reach 'beyond itself so that it may truly become a community in full communion with the other communities which form the ecclesial body of Christ and serve the mission of God' (§56). In reaching beyond, each communion looks to the other expectantly for the gifts which will build up the Body of Christ.

So, within this context, instruments of communion must proceed with subtlety and care to ensure that they serve both unity *and* diversity. Paragraph 57 remarks that there will be occasions when interim decisions

---

Instruments: A Historical and Theological Consideration of the Instruments of Communion of the Anglican Communion (London: Anglican Communion Office, 2015), 6.5.1.

[17] See Martin Luther, *Lectures on Romans*, ed. and trans. Wilhelm Pauck (Louisville: Westminster John Knox Press, 1961), drawing of course on Augustine.

may be needed. For Anglicans, this will be so not least when new questions are arising or when cultural complexity and the emerging insights of other disciplines make definitive decisions extremely difficult. Given that the communion we are called to is fundamentally eschatological in nature (§46), the relationship between patient discernment, interim decisions, and more binding definitive conclusions demands closer and deeper investigation. The classical Anglican commitment to the role of reason, alongside that of Scripture and tradition, could be helpful here, and we look to the second phase of ARCIC III to ensure that the gift of reason is properly integrated in the process of moral discernment.

WTW's reflection on the eucharist is both theological and social. It is through the celebration of the eucharist that each church shares in the *koinonia* of the body and blood of Christ (§59), and thus participates in communion with the Lord and his wider ecclesial body. As the 'fullness of ecclesial reality' (§47) is actualized, especially in eucharistic communion with the bishop, the reconciling love of Christ which overflows in 'reconciliation, justice, and peace, and witness to the joy of the resurrection' (§58) should become characteristic of Christ's followers. This is the essential root of Christian ethical behaviour. Much of the language employed in these paragraphs is reminiscent of the theological tone of classical Anglican eucharistic theology evidenced in the Book of Common Prayer. For example, we receive Christ's body and blood 'that we may evermore dwell in him, and he in us'[18] and that we may 'continue in that holy fellowship, and do all such good works as thou hast prepared for us to walk in.'[19]

Ecclesial communion: local and trans-local

Moving on from the shared ecclesiological outlines which have preceded it, this subsection provides a helpful precis of the differences between Anglicans and Roman Catholics both in emphasis and in theological understanding about the nature and structure of the Church. However, instead of seeking either to minimize or simply to note discrepancies, the document explicitly identifies these differences as areas where 'ecclesial repentance and receptive learning can take place' (§62). This is a crucial point; so often in the past, differing structures themselves have been perceived as a central part of the problem of disunity. Part of this document's genius is that what have often been considered boundary markers

---

[18] The Prayer of Humble Access.
[19] Prayer after Communion.

can instead be viewed as potential icons of mutual learning. This is a real development of trust in the Spirit of the one who has broken down the wall that separates Jews and Gentiles from each other 'in his flesh' (Eph 2.14). Here is a rich fruit of the theology of communion. If our fundamental identity is rooted in baptism, and developed in a shared theology of the Church, the basic operating system of our analysis of one another has to change as we look to one another expectant of the Holy Spirit.

For some Anglicans, the papal model of a universal teaching authority can seem quite attractive. For others, it risks annihilating diversity. However, the Archbishop of Canterbury's office (and the Anglican touchstone of communion with the See of Canterbury) is not a dissipated form of the Petrine office, as if it were possible to have a diluted form of the papacy, but rather an alternative model. It is rooted in the notion of bonds of affection which hold Anglicans together in communion, respecting the integrity and ecclesiality of each member church. As *WTW* highlights, some of the differences between Anglicans and Roman Catholics in practical expressions of decision-making and authority can be explained by reference to our separate histories (§66). It is also important to reflect on how different Anglican provinces have developed their own polities, adding further complexity to the task of discerning how the local relates to the trans-local. The heart of the question is surely 'what should be the appropriate balance between trans-local autonomy and mutual accountability' (§70), but this is greatly complicated by diverse cultural, juridical, and theological traditions within our own Communion. *WTW* reminds Anglicans that the diversity of expression within the Anglican family itself might be potential gift rather than threat, as we discern complexities which are linked to factors such as post-colonialism and modernity. In an interconnected, networked world, where social media increasingly beguile us into thinking that we know more about each other than we often do, what the document affirms as 'strong bonds of affection' and 'more robust forms of mutual accountability' (§71) are surely needed to develop a stronger theology of communion within our own tradition as well as in relation with others. Face-to-face encounters like those of the Anglican Consultative Council, the Primates' Meeting, and the Lambeth Conference remind us that these affectionate bonds are supposed to build us up in love (Col 3.14) rather than force us to submit. The simultaneously 'affective' and 'effective' characteristics of these instruments of communion are fundamentally expressions of the whole Church's pastoral office.

This section of *WTW* is a profoundly honest appraisal of current reality. Admitting that 'each tradition experiences its own particular tensions,' in the sections which follow, there is no sense of the Church as a perfect society. After all, the Co-Chairs' Preface explicitly speaks of the Church as *ecclesia 'semper reformanda'*. The instruments which govern the Church are servants of her mission and unity, and therefore 'reformable in function' (§72) for both our traditions. The document notes that '*episcope*, synodality, and primacy are enduring and necessary' (§72), but the form of these gifts can be renewed and reformed. Other instruments of communion must also be tested to ensure that they 'serve the current needs of mission and unity' (§75) which are the very centre of the Church's identity. For Anglicans, questions of how synodal structures and episcopal ministries are properly discerned, formed, and educated are urgent priorities in every context to ensure that the Gospel is proclaimed afresh in each generation. Particular care should be taken by trans-local structures in order to resist the temptation to homogenize the Church. As both our communions assess the adequacy of instruments of communion, it will be important to recognize and critique the sociological forces which encourage Christians to homogenize and flatten out distinctiveness, as well as the temptation to theologize homogeneity.

Anglicans and Roman Catholics affirm together that the episcopate is part of the *esse* of the Church. In human terms, the figure of the bishop is a relational symbol of Christ in the local church, and signifies the unity of the Church beyond the boundaries of the local and trans-local. The mutual dependence of presbyters and bishops is also a feature of much Anglican ecclesiology. Therefore, as we continue, we must be aware of the need for developing communion and coherence between instruments of communion in both our churches.

Further development of how non-Catholics might associate themselves with the ministry of the Bishop of Rome is not discussed in any detail; there is still much to harvest from *Ut Unum Sint*, *The Gift of Authority*, and *Evangelii Gaudium*. But Anglicans will be pleased to note the encouragement here to engage in intensified conversations on this issue (§76). This is surely not separate from the broader concern of how 'to contain conflict so that it does not lead to further impairment of communion' (§77). For the Petrine ministry to be a gift for Anglicans, it must protect the diversity of the Church as well as her unity. The negative reactions in some parts of the Anglican family to *The Gift of Authority* remind us of the need for further, careful work on this issue.

The end of this section reminds us that this is a document to celebrate. It does precisely what ARCIC's critics have often challenged the Commission to do. It is the beginning of an answer to the question 'So what?' posed over many years. Precisely because of the high level of agreement between our two communions on the fundamentals of the faith reached over forty years, and our insistence on the deep baptismal *koinonia* that Anglicans and Roman Catholics already share, it is now possible to receive inspiration from the other's structured lives precisely at the point where our own is weak, or 'less developed' (§79). This is *viaticum*—food and medicine for the ecclesial journey—which our pilgrim churches offer each other rather than jealously guard for themselves.

IV. Instruments of Communion at the Local Levels of Anglican and Roman Catholic Life

Section IV is in three parts: first, analysing instruments of communion which operate at a local level in both our churches; second, identifying tensions and challenges for these instruments at a local level; and third, asking how each tradition might learn from the other in areas of 'systemic stress' (§80). The section bears a close reading in full in order to appreciate the many similarities between our churches, and the complexities at play in mutual ecclesial learning. Although, strictly speaking, both communions identify the local church with the diocese, *WTW*'s insistence that theological dialogue must take seriously the 'lived reality of the structures that sustain the churches' (§80) leads the analysis to include the parish level as well as the diocese.

IV.A Instruments of communion at the local levels of Anglican and Roman Catholic life

Christian baptism makes each person a member both of the universal Church and a local church. For most people, this local church will be a parish, which is the 'normal locus of Christian formation' (§82). Through sharing in the ministry of Christ (again expressed in the threefold office of prophet, priest, and king), lay people have a responsibility with the presbyter, under the bishop, for the life of the parish. This notion of the priesthood of all believers (1 Pet 2.5–9) is expressed for Anglicans in baptism rites and ordinals, and is a fundamental ramification of both the baptismal and eucharistic ecclesiologies which have profoundly shaped contemporary Anglicanism. It was also affirmed bilaterally in the 1982 document *Baptism, Eucharist and Ministry* of the World Council of Churches, and in previous rounds of ARCIC.[20]

---

[20] For example in *The Doctrine of the Ministry* of ARCIC I (1973), where 'the priesthood of

WTW affirms that since the Second Vatican Council, Anglicans and Roman Catholics share much in common in their theologies of the whole people of God. Lay theologians are celebrated in both communions. There are, however, differences in the practical outworking of this theology. For example, the structural involvement of lay people in authoritative roles is more a feature of the Anglican tradition, and is not merely of a consultative nature, although in many parts of the world this is also developing in the Roman Catholic Church. The process of parish appointments involves lay people more frequently in the Anglican Communion, alongside processes of advertisement and interview which would be unusual in the Roman Catholic world.

Deacons and presbyters are set apart by ordination as co-workers with the bishop, and Agreed Statements on such ministries were significant achievements of ARCIC I and II. They need not be rehearsed here. In both communions, each presbyter derives their licence from the bishop, and cannot operate without one. The bishop is the principal minister of Word and sacrament in each diocese, and acts 'in service of the *koinonia* of the Church'.[21] To a very large extent, Anglicans and Roman Catholics share a theology of the episcopate. Differences in emphasis and practice emerge when *WTW* analyses how the bishop's authority operates. The Anglican relationship of 'bishop-in-synod' (§90) is not mirrored in the Roman Catholic Church, although the bishop has the discretion to summon a synod or a pastoral council. The principle of the bishop as 'sole legislator' in the Roman Catholic Church is only really paralleled in the Anglican tradition by the need for the consent of the bishop for motions of synod to be enacted.[22] One of the few moments in *WTW* where difference is perhaps understated is in the selection and appointment of bishops. While the aim of both processes is doubtless that of preserving 'the Church in a unity of faith, sacramental practice, and mission to others' (§91), there is no Anglican parallel for a universal structure of episcopal appointment as seen in the Latin rite of the Roman Catholic Church.

The integrity of each local church is a theological matter. Therefore it is only with real care and in exceptional circumstances that one see—even Canterbury—might interfere with or comment on the election of a bishop

---

all the faithful' (7) and 'the common Christian priesthood' (13) are referred to. See www.anglicancommunion.org/media/105233/ARCIC_I_The_Doctrine_of_the_Ministry.pdf.

[21] Church of England, *Bishops in Communion: Collegiality in Service of the Koinonia of the Church* (London: Church House Publishing, 2000).

[22] e.g. in the Church of England General Synod, consensus is needed in the House of Bishops before any change to matters touching on faith and order can be approved.

in another member church, as long as that bishop is recognizable as a bishop in each place.

IV.B Tensions and difficulties in the practice of communion at the local levels of Anglican and Roman Catholic life

This subsection moves on to highlight some of the challenges which mitigate against a theology of communion and its instruments. Parochialism is the first danger to emerge. Anyone who has ever worked in parish ministry will recognize how swiftly this can arise in a variety of forms, and how difficult it is to monitor. Diversity of liturgical practice is easier to monitor but just as hard to address. In the Church of England, the Fresh Expressions movement, changes within and around the parish system, and the number of churches which depart not only from the authorized rites but also from lectionaries have greatly complicated the picture. The presence of non-parochial expressions of the Church—and their growth in some dioceses in the Communion—also pose a challenge to our theology of the local parish unit. Furthermore, our liturgy images our faith. Anglicans need to ensure that liturgical renewal is pursued with great care. What we do and say in church really does matter, and is rarely neutral in whether it builds up the body of Christ. Liturgical coherence is at least as important as structural coherence, and a crisis in the one often indicates a crisis in the other.

For Anglicans the 'legislative focus' and parliamentary style of our synodical bodies can pose very serious problems, even eclipsing 'the need for catechesis and renewal' (§94). The presence of quasi-official interest groups, voting en bloc and strategically, can be especially corrosive of communion and the bonds of trust. This is a particular problem for Anglican bodies. As paragraph 94 makes clear, in the Roman Catholic Church lay participation in instruments of governance (where it occurs) is usually just consultative. It is easy for Anglicans to adopt a rather superior attitude in these circumstances. However, Anglicans might also reflect on the role that charism should play in ecclesial governance and discernment, and engage in critical reflection on what has sometimes been a rather unthinking reification of secular models.

Paragraph 95 addresses the highly complex area of alternative and parallel jurisdictions. One of the knottiest features of this question, not explicitly discussed in *WTW*, is the nature of the link between geography and episcopal leadership. What this paragraph calls 'trans-jurisdictional accountability' has sometimes been described as a consumerist approach to authority: choosing a bishop (or a community) whose views on one or other matter are acceptable to a parish or group, and thus mitigating against the catholicity of the whole. This statement is not intended to minimize either the theological problems which, in the Anglican world, have given rise to these situations or the sincerity of those taking advantage of authorized structures. It is simply to raise the question of how such jurisdictions might contribute more fully to the strengthening of the *koinonia* of the whole. As *WTW* shows, this matters to our ecumenical partners, as well as within our own provinces and the whole Anglican Communion.

The final paragraph of this subsection raises questions which emerge from changing demographics in church life. There are broad similarities here: both our communions are currently experiencing overall numerical growth, and there is some similarity in geographical patterns. However, the decision-making surrounding ecumenical 'shared ministries' in the Anglican Communion at a provincial level does open questions about how such localized decisions relate to the universal Communion, and to other bilateral ecumenical commitments made at a Communion-wide level. This is a feature of Anglican provincial autonomy which may benefit from receptive learning and further reflection.

IV.C Potential receptive ecclesial learning at the local levels of Anglican and Roman Catholic life

This next subsection moves on to discuss specific examples where there is potential for receptive ecclesial learning in the local context. The first is in the area of parallel jurisdictions. In some parts of the world, the oft-quoted Patristic principle of 'one bishop, one city'[23] has not been upheld for quite a long time. In fact, multiple jurisdictions are of course a feature of the ecumenical landscape. However, it is also the case within churches. This is perhaps most famously so in the Orthodox world: although ancient canons place orthodox 'living in non-orthodox lands' under the care of the Patriarch of Constantinople, in reality there are myriad overlapping orthodox ecclesial jurisdictions between churches in full communion. The Western pattern is less prolific: as *WTW* highlights, the presence of Eastern Catholic jurisdictions within and alongside other structures is the main example. However, in the Anglican world, the presence of the Convocation of Episcopal Churches

---

[23] See the Apostolic tradition of Hippolytus, Cyprian, and other sources from the Patristic era. St Ignatius' Epistle to the Smyrnaeans (chapter 8) assumes and defends the monoepiscopal model: 'Wherever the bishop shall appear, there let the multitude also be; even as, wherever Jesus Christ is, there is the Catholic Church.'

in Europe, alongside the Church of England Diocese in Europe, is a significant unresolved ecclesiological anomaly. Ongoing discernment is also needed in northern Europe and Scandinavia, where churches of the Porvoo Communion—with which the Anglican Communion is in a relationship of full communion—are the local church, and where there are still Anglican parishes and chaplaincies. There is also the different but related question of non-geographical jurisdiction: in the Roman Catholic Church this can be considered through the presence of ordinariate communities, and in the Church of England there are provincial episcopal visitors who care for parishes currently unable to receive the episcopal and presbyteral ministry of women.

WTW poses the question of how far parallel and overlapping jurisdictions might offer a useful model where there are culturally distinct ecclesial realities alongside one another in a relationship of full communion. Given the pace of change in contemporary culture, and the many layers of meaning freighted to conceptions of culture, it might be helpful for the Commission to consider just how far 'culture' can be pressed. How do concepts of culture contribute to our consideration of ecclesial diversity? Might a deeper sense of, and theology of, culture contribute towards our discernment of what are and what are not adiaphora? Equally importantly, the 'catholic' nature of the whole Church, and of each local expression of the Church, is guaranteed by legitimate diversity. One challenge is how to work through this exceptionally detailed material while insisting that parallel jurisdictions must always build up the unity, holiness, catholicity, and apostolicity of the local and the trans-local. *WTW*'s insistence on the premise of full communion as essential for healthy parallel jurisdictions is a helpful reminder of how destructive cross-border interventions and illegal or irregular consecrations are to the health and catholicity of the Church.

There are further lessons here for both communions, in particular in how the voices of whole parishes and communities are heard in wider discernment, and in learning from one another's structures of discernment. In situations of tension, *WTW* asks whether Anglicans would also benefit from a greater sense of a universal Anglican identity. In the reception of this document, Anglican bodies might consider how this might be achieved. As has already been highlighted, at least one communion-wide eucharistic prayer would be a rich symbol of such identity, alongside encouraging regional Anglican synods, and work on an agreed basic programme and texts for those training for ordination. Much of this can be learned by receptive reflection on Catholic practice.

19

This section closes with a strong recommendation of a greater sharing in practical *koinonia* at episcopal and parochial levels. The commissioning of the IARCCUM bishops provides a model for Anglican–Catholic episcopal shared ministry for bishops throughout our communions. The practical reception of this document will depend in part on how this shared ministry is encouraged. The upcoming Lambeth Conference in 2020 is both a great opportunity to learn from IARCCUM bishops already engaged in such work and a potential moment for the Archbishop of Canterbury to encourage such partnership as a norm throughout the Communion. However, here we must sound a small note of caution: precisely because all the baptized share in the *tria munera Christi*, this work of building communion cannot be left to the bishops alone. For our churches to genuinely walk together, it is essential that local and parish groups learn how to live the experience of real, imperfect, but deepening communion together. Whether ecclesiologies are 'bottom-up' or 'top-down', this pilgrim ethic is essential for the reception of what the Spirit appears to be saying to our churches.

V. Instruments of Communion at the Regional Levels of Anglican and Roman Catholic Life

This section follows the same pattern as the previous one. First, the document describes how instruments of communion work at a regional level in both communions. Second, it identifies areas where there is tension or stress in relation to these instruments. Finally, it asks where mutual receptive learning might take place.

The need for structures which nurture and guard the communion of the Church is rooted in and testified to in Scripture. The local synods which were features of the life of the early Church (and continued to operate regularly for many centuries in the Christian East) reveal a concern for how local churches relate to one another. Instruments of communion are supposed to allow for—and protect—subsidiarity, that principle which determines that decisions should be made at the lowest appropriate level. By inference, there will always be some decisions which relate to issues touching on the wider Church, which need to be tested by reference to wider Christian discernment. Anglicans will be familiar with the principle of subsidiarity through the *Virginia Report* and *Windsor Report* and the Covenant process. It is intended to protect the theological and cultural integrity of the local, while prompting a simultaneous exercise of wisdom which builds up the whole.

V.A The nature and instruments of communion at the regional levels of Anglican and Roman Catholic life

Despite the many differences between Anglicans and Roman Catholics in the nature and exercise of instruments of communion at this level, *WTW* speaks of a 'familial resemblance' (§109) which stems from a common heritage in the early and medieval Church. This is appropriate language for those who speak of one another in fraternal terms, and helpfully roots our two communions in shared territory.

At this stage it is essential to highlight that many of the differences in structure and pattern do not always stem from theological conviction. The patterns of empire and missionary expansion, and their bequeathed models, are as much cultural phenomena as anything else. While Anglicans now largely think of 'national' churches, the document explains how Roman Catholics have largely been cautious in promoting this language. The history of much of the Anglican Communion is greatly influenced by the history of colonialism and independence, although there are churches such as the Scottish Episcopal Church which are not shaped by this inheritance in such a direct way. The document mentions the first Lambeth Conference in 1868, convened to address 'questions of mission, unity, faith, and order arising within and among the regional churches' (§110). The third Lambeth Conference of 1888 then adopted what we now know as the Lambeth Quadrilateral—a version of a proposal first shaped by the Episcopal priest and ecumenical pioneer William Reed Huntington, who hoped that Anglicanism could become the basis of 'a church of the reconciliation'[24]—which commits the Communion to four points: first, that the Holy Scriptures are the ultimate rule of faith; second, the sufficiency of the Apostles' and Niceno-Constantinopolitan Creeds; third, the dominical sacraments of baptism and eucharist, and fourth, the historic episcopate, 'locally adapted in the methods of its administration to the varying needs of the nations and people called of God into the Unity of His Church'.[25] These principles have underpinned Anglican identity and the maintenance of communion between the regional churches ever since.

Basic Anglican polity allows for greater diversity and depth of decision-making within the province than is currently the case in the Roman Catholic Church. Each Anglican province has its own legal constitution and synodical structures which include clergy and laity. Even the precise

---

[24] See Paul Avis, *Anglicanism and the Christian Church* (London and New York: T & T Clark, 2002), p. 350.
[25] See Randall Davidson (ed.), *The Five Lambeth Conferences* (London: SPCK, 1920), pp. 122–3.

nature of synodal or conventional presidency varies.[26] There is less diversity in the Latin Catholic rite, although the document helpfully points out that two recent documents of Pope Francis have attempted to strengthen the trans-local or regional level of ecclesial decision-making (§110). This section contains useful points of clarification for both Anglicans and Roman Catholics about their own and one another's local structures. These are detailed in paragraphs 111–14. It also helps us avoid caricature: for example, Pope Francis's *de facto* recognition of the intrinsic authority of teaching documents from particular episcopal conferences by referring to them in his encyclicals shows a dynamic relationship between the local church and the universal Church which is often missed.

Two features stand out which, in the broad context of the document, are perhaps worthy of individual comment from an Anglican perspective. The Roman Catholic practice of regional episcopal synods, attended also by representatives of the competent Vatican department, is one which could greatly strengthen the Anglican world. Something similar happens with the Council of Anglican Provinces of Africa (CAPA), but this pattern could be explored much more widely. Secondly, it is important to note that local primacy of a senior bishop is a feature of both of our communions. Although this is lived out in slightly diverse ways in international Anglicanism, it is of profound importance for the prayerful maintenance of communion and the public face of the Church.

V.B Tensions and difficulties in the practice of communion at the regional levels of Anglican and Roman Catholic life

The stresses and difficulties in building communion at a regional level are very different for Anglicans and Roman Catholics. Anglicans are often excessively bound by what might be seen as mimicking a parliamentary or democratic model, whereas Roman Catholics are defined by a system where authority is strongly centralized. In the Anglican world, often our synodical structures can ensure a fairly monochrome membership. The social background and age of those elected to representative bodies are examples of topics which may need to be addressed in parts of the Anglican world. When cultural and political contexts outweigh broader theological discernment within a provincial body, these must be tested in the wider church. The role of the episcopate as the ministry specifically charged with teaching the faith and guarding this treasure can sometimes be obscured through quasi-parliamentary procedure (§116). Better

---

[26] See §111.

theologies of charism and cultures could be of great service to both our communions, and may even assist in discerning future patterns of non-adversarial practice in ecclesial decision-making.

V.C Potential receptive ecclesial learning at the regional levels of Anglican and Roman Catholic life

The final paragraphs of this section make some practical suggestions as to how each communion might learn from the life of the other. Once again, *WTW* affirms that despite 'noticeable asymmetry' (§119) between our structures, these differences are part of the context in which we together learn the life of communion. In other words, our structural differences can be considered laboratories of the Spirit as we grow in unity. We must not underestimate what a profound theological development this is, rooted in ARCIC's heritage of reflection on the Gospels and ancient common traditions, and enabled by the substantial but imperfect communion that our churches already share in the life of faith.

Anglicans are challenged to learn from the self-conscious universality of the Roman Catholic Church. The process surrounding the proposed Anglican Communion Covenant has revealed a significant degree of resistance to anything which might question provincial autonomy. But here, the suggestions are not principally juridical, but couched in the language of representation and mutual accountability and responsibility. The possibility of 'mutual visitation' between dioceses/provinces offers a helpful model which, through its face-to-face nature, might help reduce unhelpful caricature or generalization.

The document also suggests that Anglicans might receive some help in strengthening our sense of corporate episcopal authority. The oft-repeated totem that Anglicanism is 'episcopally governed and synodically led' is rarely unpacked. The question of what kind of theological density belongs to a college of bishops in a province or an episcopal conference is one for both communions. The opportunity for Anglican colleges of bishops to teach with a united voice in their own contexts is one which would further strengthen communion with other provinces. The unified voice of an episcopate also has a missionary dimension, through which episcopal teaching has more weight in its wider national and international surroundings. Finally, in the many and diverse complex situations currently facing the Anglican Communion, the encouragement to include consultant experts in discernment and study is a much-needed one. For example, debates surrounding the human person should be carefully informed by up-to-date expertise in science and social science.

There are challenges, too, for Roman Catholics which an Anglican commentary should mention very briefly. The document encourages Roman Catholics to learn from the 'characteristic theology and associated principles of the provincial church' and to develop a 'pastoral magisterium' which takes local context and need very seriously (§120). Pope Francis's document *Amoris Laetitia* is quoted several times, revealing what a rich source it is for ecclesiology as well as for ethics. Much of *WTW* is about the dynamics of relationship between and within the churches. It is an encouragement for Anglicans to read how Roman Catholics might learn from the Anglican provincial model about how bishops' conferences might appropriately question 'initiatives and directives emanating from Rome' (§121).

It is an immense challenge for both our churches to outline a theologically mature, affective, and effective relationship between the local, trans-local, and universal which is able to take diverse culture seriously. Together, we are part of a living tradition which has itself evolved, changed, and developed over many centuries. For Anglicans, the further development of deliberative and reflective structures which are authoritative without always needing to be decisive is a particular challenge. Learning carefully from other traditions in which we know the Holy Spirit is operative is a fundamental part of that journey. At a provincial level, especially where bodies are more or less coterminous, a commitment to such mutual learning could be evidenced by a commitment to regular joint statements by episcopal conferences and houses of bishops on national or regional matters. In strengthening the communion of the regional, we strengthen the communion of the whole Church, and it is to the universal level that we must now turn.

VI. Instruments of Communion at the Worldwide/ Universal Level of Anglican and Roman Catholic Life

This section follows the same trifold pattern as Sections IV and V. As well as offering an analysis of structures with the intention of mutual learning, this material is a helpful precis for Anglicans wanting to learn more about their own tradition. Both Roman Catholic and Anglican patterns of oversight are discussed with clarity and focus.

The conciliar document *Unitatis Redintegratio* celebrates the common heritage preserved in Anglican institutions[27] as well as in the content

---

[27] Decree on Ecumenism *Unitatis Redintegratio* §13, in Vatican Council II, ed. Flannery, p. 513.

of the faith itself. The 'service rendered by instruments of communion' towards the maintenance of faith and communion can be considered among such institutions (§123). While structures of oversight have developed over time, the Anglican experience has been to emphasize provincial autonomy, while creating dynamic structures of accountability which ensure doctrinal cohesion across the Communion. The Roman Catholic experience has been far more attuned to normative universal governance.

Neither of these experiences is perhaps fully balanced, and both therefore have something of what we might call an ecclesial deficit.[28] Paragraph 124 outlines differences in Anglican and Roman Catholic self-understanding of how each Church relates to the one, holy, catholic, and apostolic Church of Christ. The Anglican pattern of what has been called a 'modesty' in our ecclesiology[29] shines through here. Anglicans do not make exclusive ecclesiological claims. The lines of demarcation indicated by the Lambeth Quadrilateral allow space for the development of an indigenous, provincial Catholicism, where there is a communion of churches guaranteed by 'mutual loyalty sustained through the common counsel of the bishops in conference'.[30]

VI.A The nature and instruments of communion at the worldwide levels of Anglican and Roman Catholic life

This subsection articulates very clearly the differences in our ecclesiological praxis. Although since the *Virginia Report* and *Windsor Report*, and the beginning of the Covenant process, there has been much more consideration of how 'centralized' instruments of communion might operate, the default operational mode of Anglicanism remains provincial. Equally, it might be said that although since the Second Vatican Council there has been much more emphasis on conciliarity and synodality, the default mode of Roman Catholicism remains a centralized authority. Both habits are placed under analysis and scrutiny in *WTW*.

It emerges that the 'character of decisions' at a universal level varies markedly. No centralized Anglican decision (whether a Lambeth Conference resolution, a document of the Primates' Meeting, or a resolution by the Anglican Consultative Council) can be considered binding on the provinces. Bonds which are principally affectionate cannot be juridical

---

28 This notion has been discussed in the Anglican context by the Windsor Continuation Group.
29 Modesty as a characteristic in Anglican theology and ecclesiology has been elaborated on in contemporary writing about the Church; see Paul Avis, *The Identity of Anglicanism: Essentials of Anglican Ecclesiology* (London: Continuum, 2007) for a good recent example.
30 The report of the 1930 Lambeth Conference, quoted in *WTW* §130.

in quite that way, even if they do have a moral force. While most magisterial teaching 'at the universal level is not definitive' (§126) for Roman Catholics, there is a stronger sense of a centralized power in Rome which is perhaps rooted both in the ancient power of the Roman See as a seat of final appeal and in the nature of the Latin legal tradition.

However, both our traditions teach that conciliarity and primacy belong together, and that a delicate, dynamic balance (see §127) is needed between the two for the Church to be healthy. Each province experiences this reality in some form, and it is perhaps at these two poles of conciliarity and primacy where mutual, receptive learning can most fruitfully occur.

Participation in a General Council has not been possible for Anglicans since the Reformation. Elsewhere, questions have been raised by both Anglicans and Roman Catholics on just how much could be required of Anglicans in a future united Christendom, particularly with regard to topics that were defined in an earlier situation of ecclesial division. Many Anglicans celebrate the documents of the Second Vatican Council precisely because it was a pastoral council without anathemas. Even without councils, both communions affirm that guarding the deposit of faith and expressing the *sensus fidelium* are the principal responsibility of bishops. The Synod of Bishops, the Lambeth Conference, and the Primates' Meeting all testify to this in slightly different ways. However, both communions would also now affirm that conciliarity is not just the responsibility of the episcopate. The 2006 Agreed Statement between Orthodox and Anglicans, *The Church of the Triune God*, expressed the clear ecclesiological importance of this realization: '... we must approach the concept of the college of bishops with great care: it must not be allowed to undermine the basic principles of synodality by detaching the bishops from their church communities, and setting the college of bishops over against the Church as a whole.'[31] There are implications here for both Anglicans and Roman Catholics in considering how the diverse and symphonic voice of the whole Church—including lay people, theologians, and those whose voices are easily and unintentionally marginalized—is discerned and articulated. The Anglican Consultative Council is the only Anglican instrument of communion where there is guaranteed lay representation. This guards against any temptation to see role of the laity as simply those who utter an 'Amen' to episcopal discernment, but a theology of the Council (particularly as related to the Primates' Meeting and Lambeth Conference) is

---

[31] International Commission for Anglican–Orthodox Theological Dialogue, *The Church of the Triune God*, The Cyprus Statement (London: The Anglican Communion Office, 2006), V: 25.

underdeveloped. Work on this area could potentially be helpful for both Anglicans and Roman Catholics as we consider together structures of authority and *koinonia*.

There are very marked differences in how our two communions practise primacy. At first glance, paragraph 133 may appear rather too short to introduce a topic of this magnitude. However, *WTW* enters this conversation informed by the mature and serious work of two previous commissions: the thorough bibliography points the reader towards much of this material. One charism which is perhaps shared by both the Pope and the Archbishop of Canterbury is that of convening other instruments of communion. Both are personal, visible ministries and are related to *sees* which have particular historic resonance. One is juridically guaranteed, whereas the other has the informal moral authority of one who is *primus inter pares*. However, it is clear that forms of primacy are essential to guarantee diversity and to draw plurality into communion.

VI.B Tensions and difficulties in the practice of communion at the worldwide/universal levels of Anglican and Roman Catholic life

Both our communions are currently finding that structures which are supposed to serve the unity of a diverse—and continually diversifying— ecclesial body are under significant stress. What some sociologists have referred to as 'a crisis of institutions' is also by no means simply the preserve of the churches. However, there are particular tensions for Anglicans which can appear insoluble. Broadly speaking, autonomous provinces which claim interdependence are experiencing 'strain on the bonds of affection and the capacity of the instruments of communion to respond' (§137). Paragraph 137 of the document helpfully reminds the reader that many provincial changes in ethical teaching are made in response to what the local church believes to be the demands of mission. While not removing the difficulties associated with such changes, this does remind us that others do not seek to tear the fabric of communion, but rather to act with integrity in their own context. The various listening exercises currently taking place within Anglican provinces, particularly on the topic of human sexuality, are seeking to understand this more deeply. However, ultimate questions remain as to how matters are discerned to be Church-dividing, and what 'universal' responses are appropriate in such cases.

Universal gatherings of the episcopate are fraught for various and diverse reasons. The numerical growth in the episcopate of the Roman Catholic Church makes it hard to imagine a General Council. The Synod of Bishops in the Roman Catholic Church is under ongoing development as a theological body, but its methodology is contested, and its authority is unclear. The Lambeth Conference is still able to operate as a universal gathering of Anglican bishops, but has no formal teaching authority, and its ability to exercise discernment and promote communion is damaged when provinces refuse to attend. However, it is important to affirm the intrinsic authority of such a gathering. That the Conference is 'a body composed of those who by their ordination to the episcopate have been given apostolic responsibility to govern means that the resolutions of a Lambeth Conference may be considered to have an intrinsic authority which is inherent in their members gathered together'.[32] The Primates' Meeting has perhaps the greatest potential for acting as a body in which primacy-in-communion can be exercised, but in both cases that which is inherent and implicit needs further investigation and articulation.

There is little theological parity between the primacy of the Bishop of Rome, with powers of immediate and ordinary jurisdiction, and the informal, moral convening powers of the Archbishop of Canterbury. However, unity in both our communions is guaranteed by a relationship of communion with each of these primatial figures and their sees. Alongside mutual learning on conciliarity, this pole of primacy is perhaps a helpful place for further reflection to begin on mutual learning. As *WTW* attests, Pope Francis has encouraged local bishops and episcopal conferences to be much more conscious of their own implicit theological authority, without frequently deferring to Rome.

While very few in the Anglican Communion would advocate moving beyond a primacy of honour for the Archbishop of Canterbury, how archbishops of Canterbury exercise a servant ministry which builds up love and nourishes the bonds of affection for the sake of communion needs further consideration with or without a formal Covenant to establish it.

VI.C Potential receptive ecclesial learning at the worldwide levels of Anglican and Roman Catholic life

WTW affirms that both communions have much to learn from each other. The close relationship of communion which we already celebrate is one that should liberate us from insecurity and nervousness in mutual learning. From an Anglican perspective, the Roman Catholic Church has been operating at an international level for much longer than the Anglican

---

[32] Windsor Continuation Group Report, in *One Love: The Official Report of ACC-14* (London: Anglican Consultative Council, 2010), §66.

Communion, and there are surely gifts to be received without ecclesiological mimicry. This subsection of *WTW* deserves close scrutiny. More than this, it is urgent that its many points of practical suggestion are examined and received by the relevant authorities in both our churches. This commentary will focus on points of potential Anglican learning.

The Covenant process has revealed the extent to which a majority of Anglicans appear to be allergic to greater centralized control. However, the communion theology which underpins both substantial ecumenical progress and the life of our own denomination itself has great implications for how we order our common life. There is a clarity which emerges from *koinonia* in a form of responsibility for one another in the household of faith.

Some of *WTW*'s recommendations are rooted in remembrance. How do we remain conscious of one another especially at moments of great celebration of tension? The liturgy is fundamental to this process. Thus a common eucharistic prayer (§145), commended to be used in every province perhaps at major occasions, preferably with the name of the local bishop and possibly the name of the Archbishop of Canterbury commemorated within the anaphora, would be both a means and an expression of our universal communion. We could also remember one another in common calendars and catechisms. None of this work should be understood as threatening to the ecclesiological autonomy of each province, and it needs to be pursued intentionally at a Communion-wide level. The formal reception of the 2008 document *The Principles of Canon Law Common to the Churches of the Anglican Communion* is also recommended by the Commission.

The emphasis on service in the ministry of Pope Francis, his consistent references to the principle of subsidiarity, and his reluctance to close down debate might help Anglicans reconsider how a Communion-wide ministry of oversight from the Archbishop of Canterbury might be received. Again, it is worth stressing again for both our communions that conciliarity and primacy must always be held together, and while it would be ludicrous for the role of the Archbishop of Canterbury to develop on quasi-papal lines in terms of jurisdiction, patriarchal language has been used of the office of Archbishop in previous ecumenical conversations,[33] and a personal min-

---

[33] Cardinal Mercier of Mechlen-Bruxelles made this suggestion when considering how the Church of England could be 'united but not absorbed' with the Catholic Church through the Malines Conversations of the early twentieth century. The 'uniate' nature of such a suggestion would now be considered eccentric and implausible by many theologians. However, fresh insight could be gained into the Archbishop of Canterbury's role in the wider Anglican

istry which serves the unity of a relatively new ecclesial communion is a gift which could be further explored and carefully tested in the light of this receptive methodology. This dynamic between the poles of conciliarity and primacy creates a certain amount of space where issues can be discerned over time, impacts of change assessed, and warnings given. In such a context, the ministry of the Archbishop could further develop without a self-conscious disciplinary charism into 'a paradigm of episcopal oversight that is personal and pastoral and that guides, leads and challenges'.[34]

The See of Canterbury and its cathedral, intrinsically linked to the ministry of the Archbishop of Canterbury as an instrument of communion, also have a role in supporting the development and maintenance of communion. Even in an age where technology offers so many possibilities, the realities of face-to-face encounter cannot be underestimated, especially when affection itself needs to be strengthened. Could there be several specific Sundays during the year where different Anglican primates, or new bishops, are invited to preside at the main eucharist in Canterbury Cathedral? Could funding be found for every new bishop in the Communion to visit Canterbury at least once in their first three years of office? Regional or topic-based synods as recommended in paragraph 145 could also strengthen a sense of collegiality among the bishops and fellowship among other participants within the Anglican Communion. Full and regular participation in such a synodal process by Roman Catholic bishops would also aid the development of *koinonia* between our communions. It is not principally for an Anglican commentator to suggest how the Roman Catholic Church might respond to this, but a new category of ecumenical cardinals would be an extraordinary sign of universal commitment to the goal of full, visible unity. Anglican participation in *ad limina* visits really ought to become a normal feature of such occasions (see §147), properly coordinated between the relevant authorities.

Towards the end of this final section, there is an extremely important short paragraph on the principle of re-reception (§149). Especially when communions have developed apart from one other, attention to the dynamic of re-reception is fundamental. *The Gift of Authority*, published in 1999, states, 'The churches suffer when some element of ecclesial communion has been forgotten, neglected or abused ... Thus, there may be a

---

Communion through conscious and careful consideration of how a patriarchal model, informed by other such offices in both East and West, might be a legitimate development in Anglican polity for the sake of the whole.

[34] Inter-Anglican Standing Commission on Unity, Faith and Order, *Towards a Symphony of Instruments*, 3.4.7, quoted in *WTW* §135.

rediscovery of elements that were neglected and a fresh remembrance of the promises of God, leading to a renewal of the Church's "Amen".[35] A recognition that the Holy Spirit has not abandoned Christian communities without the inspiration of divine grace, even when they have been separated from one another for so long, reveals a rich series of ecclesiological ramifications. This is a question not only of learning from past experience or even current reality, but also about how each church might be receiving particular eschatological insight which can be discerned and shared with the other. Such gifts, and the structures they shape, are gifts of communion for the whole Church from the *eschaton*, revealing something of God's ultimate intention for creation and for the diverse body which participates in Christ's mission. There is a huge amount in this section to inspire internal housekeeping *within* both our churches. But the establishment of a small mandated body—perhaps a subsection of IARCCUM—to monitor and encourage the process of re-reception in the cause of intensifying communion *between* our churches would be of significant benefit as our journey together continues to deepen.

---

35 ARCIC II, *The Gift of Authority (Authority in the Church III)* (London: CTS; Toronto: Anglican Book Centre; and New York: Church Publishing Incorporated, 1999), §25, available at: www.vatican.va/roman_curia/pontifical_councils/chrstuni/documents/rc_pc_chrstuni_doc_12051999_gift-of-autority_en.html.

Conclusion

WTW opens up a whole new vista in Anglican–Roman Catholic relations. In its recommendations on mutual learning from one another's structures, there is an implicit recognition of ecclesiality and partnership in the Gospel. This is a dynamic relationship in which neither partner remains unchanged, because there can be no reverse gear in the process of walking together towards the goal of full, visible, eucharistic unity. The vision of conciliarity and primacy held together, and the many levels of agreement recorded in this Joint Statement, deserve to be received urgently by both our communions. For Anglicans, the Lambeth Conference of 2020 provides an obvious and timely moment to formally receive this work and to discern how our own structures might put this mutual receptive learning into practice.

There is also further theological spade-work to be done. The document recognizes that because our traditions broke apart only in the sixteenth century, in many ways 'structures and procedures' remain similar (§152). While in many ways this is of course true, it is also risky to assume that there was monochrome, uncontested structural uniformity throughout the Catholic West in the centuries prior to the Reformation. Further work and reflection on pre-Reformation diversity of structures and practice could be illuminating for contemporary ecclesiology. Equally, there is further work to be done on the charisms of discernment, and in particular on how lay people participate in that beyond simply uttering a doxological 'Amen!' to episcopal judgement.[36] The question of universal primacy continues to concern many Anglicans, and further work is needed here alongside better reception of ARCIC's previous work in this area. In particular, urgent consideration should be given to how theological colleges, seminaries, and university faculties work with this material.

This document repeatedly makes it clear that the Church's structures exist to enable her mission. In other words, they should reveal, enable, and guard the Church's inner dynamic reality in its engagement with a rapidly changing world. Such structures are therefore in need of constant renewal and refreshment to ensure that they are fit to serve the Church's communion and to engage fully with the context of contemporary culture.

---

[36] See the end of both §§156 and 157.

They are, to quote the document, essential but 'also open to reform' (§152). There are serious implications for how and when authoritative statements are made by each communion. If 'Catholics and Anglicans must give attention to what the Spirit may be saying in the other tradition before arriving at a definitive conclusion for their own particular tradition' (§153), we must hold one another to account, in love, when it appears that legitimate discussion on contested issues is being foreshortened or closed down. A passage from an Anglican consecration sermon from an earlier period of conflict in the Church of England offers a beautiful and poetic image from the prophet Ezekiel as to how a bishop might discern the complexity surrounding his church. Like the Living Creatures of Ezekiel, the bishop must have eyes all round him, 'in every member of his body ... in his head to understand his place and function ... eyes in his feet, to have a care in his goings ... eyes all round him [that] he may wink at some things out of human frailty, and possibly connive at others out of just necessity, yet will he still have one eye open to have a care upon the main.'[37] Complex situations often need discernment over time, and our instruments of communion should also liberate us from the urge to foreshorten debate for the sake of temporary clarity.

If ecclesial *structures* exist to exhibit something of ecclesial *life*, the broader *life* of the other church is surely also something from which we each need to prayerfully receive. Furthermore, if church structures reveal something of the inner reality of each church's life, Anglicans might legitimately suggest that questions about ecclesiality need to be posed afresh. To what extent can it be said that the one Church of Christ 'subsists in' the Anglican Communion? What really is the difference between a church and an 'ecclesial community'? Have we reached a point when our reflection on one another's structures has opened new insights into this matter?

One of the ongoing challenges to this work for both our communions is to engage openly and hopefully with some of the fresh questions being posed by science, social science, and cultural theory. *WTW* shows the Commission's consciousness of the need to seek out ways in which new questions can patiently be handled, without always rushing to final conclusions. A permanent Anglican–Roman Catholic group of theologians could potentially be mandated to deal with such questions. From an Anglican perspective, if we believe that the world is the locus of God's redeeming action in Christ, it is essential to discern voices of passion, expertise, and

---

37 Peter Heylyn, *Sermon on Acts 20:30–31* (London, 1659). This was preached at the consecration of Bishop John Towers in March 1639.

insight beyond the Church's structures as well as within them. This document offers wonderful reflections on mutual learnings from one another's structures; it is to be hoped that such an open disposition might enable joint, careful, even receptive listening together to wider culture in the next phase of the Commission's work.

This is a wonderfully strong document, affirming that our structures need reform as well as refreshment. As we walk together along the way, growing in unity, faith, and love, can the Anglican Communion now humbly and seriously engage in the theological questions raised by this methodology? In international terms, we are a young communion of churches, with the opportunity to learn from our older sisters and brothers in careful and prayerful discernment as we proceed along the road of 'penitence and renewal towards full communion' (§161). Increasingly, if we walk together, we will need to eat together. It remains for the process of ongoing reception, mutual accountability, and dialogue to not flee from the difficult question of whether we should therefore allow one another's eucharists to be viaticum for this journey. In St John's Gospel, Jesus says, 'Whoever eats me will live because of me' (Jn 6.57). Only thus will we ultimately grow together into the fullness of Christ.

Bibliography

ARCIC I, *The Doctrine of the Ministry* (1973), available at: www. anglicancommunion.org/media/105233/ARCIC_I_The_Doctrine_of_the_ Ministry.pdf.

ARCIC II, *The Gift of Authority (Authority in the Church III)* (London: CTS; Toronto: Anglican Book Centre; and New York: Church Publishing Incorporated, 1999), available at: www.vatican.va/roman_curia/pontifical_councils/chrstuni/ documents/rc_pc_chrstuni_doc_12051999_gift-of-autority_en.html.

Avis, Paul, *Anglicanism and the Christian Church* (London and New York: T & T Clark, 2002).

Avis, Paul, *The Identity of Anglicanism: Essentials of Anglican Ecclesiology* (London: Continuum, 2007).

The Book of Common Prayer (Cambridge: Cambridge University Press, 2004).

Church of England, *Bishops in Communion: Collegiality in Service of the Koinonia of the Church* (London: Church House Publishing, 2000).

Davidson, Randall (ed.), *The Five Lambeth Conferences* (London: SPCK, 1920).

Denaux, Adelbert, Nicholas Sagovsky, and Charles Sherlock (eds), *Looking Towards a Church Fully Reconciled* (London: SPCK, 2016).

Goulder, Michael, *A Tale of Two Missions* (Louisville: Westminster John Knox Press, 1995).

Heylyn, Peter, *Sermon on Acts 20: 30–31* (London, 1659).

Hill, Christopher, and Edward Yarnold (eds), *Anglicans and Roman Catholics: The Search for Unity* (London: SPCK, 1994).

Inter-Anglican Standing Commission on Unity, Faith and Order, *Towards a Symphony of Instruments: A Historical and Theological Consideration of the Instruments of Communion of the Anglican Communion* (London: Anglican Communion Office, 2015).

Inter-Anglican Theological and Doctrinal Commission, *The Virginia Report* (London: Anglican Consultative Council, 1997), available at: www.anglican-communion.org/media/150889/report-1.pdf.

International Commission for Anglican–Orthodox Theological Dialogue, *The Church of the Triune God*, The Cyprus Statement (London: The Anglican Communion Office, 2006).

Lambeth Commission on Communion, *The Windsor Report* (London: The Anglican Communion Office, 2004), available at: www.anglicancommunion. org/media/68225/windsor2004full.pdf.

The Lambeth Conference: Resolutions Archive from 1988, available at: http://www. anglicancommunion.org/media/127749/1988.pdf.

Luther, Martin, *Lectures on Romans*, ed. and trans. Wilhelm Pauck (Louisville: Westminster John Knox Press, 1961).

May They All Be One, House of Bishops Occasional Paper (Church House Publishing, 1997).

Minear, Paul, *Images of the Church in the New Testament* (Philadelphia: Westminster, 1960).Murphy-O'Connor, Cardinal Cormac, 'ARCIC—Dead in the Water or Money in the Bank?', Richard Stewart Lecture, Worth Abbey, 2009, available at: www.catholicnews.org.uk/Home/News/2009/Cardinal-Cormac-Murphy-O-Connor-delivers-lecture-on-ecumenism.

Murray, Paul D. (ed.), *Receptive Ecumenism and the Call to Catholic Learning* (Oxford: Oxford University Press, 2008).

One Love: Report of ACC-14 (London: Anglican Consultative Council, 2010).

Pope Benedict XVI and the Archbishop of Canterbury, His Grace Rowan Williams, 'Common Declaration' (23 November 2006), available at: http://w2.vatican.va/content/benedict-xvi/en/speeches/2006/november/documents/hf_ben-xvi_spe_20061123_common-decl.html.

Pope John Paul II, Address to ARCIC I, Castelgandolfo, 4 September 1980, available at: https://w2.vatican.va/content/john-paul-ii/en/speeches/1980/september/documents/hf_jp-ii_spe_19800904_cattolici-anglicani.html.

Pope John Paul II, *Ut Unum Sint*. Encyclical on Commitment to Ecumenism (1995), available at: http://w2.vatican.va/content/john-paul-ii/en/encyclicals/documents/hf_jp-ii_enc_25051995_ut-unum-sint.html.

Primates of the Anglican Communion, *Deeper Communion; Gracious Restraint: A Letter from Alexandria to the Churches of the Anglican Communion*, available at: http://anglicancommunion.org/media/68372/Pastoral-Letter.pdf.

Ramsey, Michael, *The Gospel and the Catholic Church* (London: Longman, 1936).

Vatican Council II: Constitutions, Decrees, Declarations, ed. Austin Flannery OP (New York: Costello, 2007).

Williams, Rowan, Willebrands Lecture, Rome, 2009, available at: http://aoc2013.brix.fatbeehive.com/articles.php/766/archbishops-address-at-a-willebrands-symposium-in-rome.